Contents

List of Figures

The **British** War on Terror

*Terrorism and Counter-terrorism on the
Home Front Since 9/11*

Steve Hewitt

continuum

Continuum International Publishing Group

The Tower Building	80 Maiden Lane
11 York Road	Suite 704
London SE1 7NX	New York NY 10038

www.continuumbooks.com

First published 2008
Reprinted 2010, 2011 (twice)

British Library Cataloguing-in-Publication Data
A catalogue record for this book is available from the British Library.

ISBN: HB: 978-0-8264-9899-1
        PB: 978-0-8264-9900-4

Library of Congress Cataloging-in-Publication Data
Hewitt, Steve.
    The British war on terror : terrorism and counter-terrorism on the home front since 9-11 / Steve Hewitt.
        p. cm.
    Includes bibliographical references.
    ISBN 978-0-8264-9899-1 -- ISBN 978-0-8264-9900-4 1. Terrorism--Great Britain. 2. Terrorism--Government policy--Great Britain. 3. Terrorism--Great Britain--Prevention. 4. London Terrorist Bombings, London, England, 2005. I. Title.
    HV6433.G7H48 2008
    363.3250941--dc22

                                                                    2007031485

Typeset by Kenneth Burnley, Wirral, Cheshire
Printed and bound in Great Britain

List of Tables

Dedicated to C. M.
for guiding me to a new life

Acknowledgements

First and foremost, this book would not have been possible without the vision and faith invested in it by Rebecca Vaughan-Williams of Continuum. Also making it happen was Andrew Christian Emery, who took time out of his busy PhD schedule to provide invaluable research assistance and feedback. Friends, Ceri Morgan, Scott Lucas and Maria Ryan, supplied crucial and expert editorial feedback. The errors that remain, hopefully small in number, are mine alone. Thanks, as well, to Peter Gill and Milena Buyum who answered queries of mine at various points during this project and to Gaye Bye and Margaret Conway for their constant help and encouragement. Finally, I would like to thank those who kept me sane in the course of an intense period of research and writing. Topping the list is the Waterloo Road Single Parents' Club (Michele, Jules and Kate) who over copious amounts of good cheer made me an honorary member of their exclusive association. My employer, the University of Birmingham, has provided me with crucial support for which I am grateful, although the views expressed in this book are mine alone. Lastly, there are my wonderful children, Isaac and Flora, who constantly remind me of life's true priorities. I apologize for the time that this book has taken me away from you. Hopefully, your world of the twenty-first century will be one where all forms of terrorism become a distant memory.

2001

19 February – The Terrorism Act 2000 comes into effect replacing the Prevention of Terrorism Act that had been in place since 1974.

7 June – Tony Blair and the Labour Party are re-elected in the general election.

11 September – Attacks occur in New York and Washington DC killing just under 3,000 people, including 67 Britons.

21 September – Lotfi Raissi, an Algerian flight instructor living in Britain, is arrested on suspicion of having been involved in the 11 September attacks. He is sent to Belmarsh Prison for several months. On 21 April 2003, all charges against him are dropped.

7 October – British and American air attacks against the Taliban in Afghanistan begin.

12 November – The Blair government introduces the Anti-Terrorism, Crime and Security bill in the House of Commons.

13 December – The Anti-Terrorism, Crime and Security Act receives royal assent.

19 December – Raids in Luton, London and the West Midlands leads to the detention of eight individuals with alleged ties to international terrorism under the new Anti-Terrorism, Crime and Security Act.

22 December – British citizen Richard Reid is arrested after he attempts to destroy American Airlines Flight 63 with an explosive hidden in his shoe.

2002

15 February – Home Secretary David Blunkett ends efforts to extradite accused terrorist Abdelghani Ait Haddad because of concern about the legitimacy of the evidence against him.

7 May – Lord Rooker, a Home Office minister, says that since the Terrorism Act 2000 came into effect on 19 February 2001 '144 persons have been arrested under [it]. There have as yet been no convictions for terrorist offences to date but ten people are undergoing or awaiting trial for such offences'.

6 July – The *Guardian* reports that the British Air Transport Association opposes a Home Office plan to require airlines to record personal information.

23 July – The date of the so-called 'Downing Street Memo'. The document reveals that the Bush administration was set by this date on war with Iraq.

30 July – The Special Immigration Appeals Commission rules that indefinite internment under Part 4 of the Anti-Terrorism, Crime and Security Act 2001 is both 'unlawful' and 'discriminatory'.

2 August – The Home Office lists two new Codes of Practice under the Regulation of Investigatory Powers Act 2000 related to intelligence collection.

9 August – An Old Bailey jury acquits Suleyman Zainulabdin, a London chef, who was arrested the previous October and charged under the Terrorism Act 2000 with 'inviting another to receive instruction or training in making or using firearms or explosives'.

22 August – The UK Home Office issues a Circular (44/2002) authorizing police and other authorities to request airline and shipping companies to provide 'police intelligence' on passengers.

5 September – Amnesty International issues a report expressing concern 'about serious human rights violations that have taken place as a consequence of the United Kingdom (UK) authorities' response to the 11 September 2001 attacks in the United States of America'.

12 October – Bombs explode in the Indonesian resort of Bali killing 202 people. Twenty-four Britons are among the dead.

2003

5 January – Police arrest seven men in London related to a plot to manufacture the poison ricin for attacks on the London Underground. All were later acquitted of murder charges related to the ricin plot, although another would be convicted of 'conspiracy to commit a public nuisance by the use of poisons or explosives to cause disruption, fear or injury'.

14 January – Police raid a flat in Manchester while searching for a terrorism suspect. In the course of being arrested, Kamel Bourgass, one of the ricin suspects, stabs to death Detective Constable Stephen Oake.

20 January – Police raid the Finsbury Park mosque. They arrest seven people and seize weapons and forged passports.

30 January – Richard Reid, the 'shoe bomber', is convicted of terrorism by an American court and sentenced to life in prison.

5 February – During a public briefing to the United Nations Security Council, Colin Powell makes reference to the ricin arrests in the UK the month before and implicitly links these to the Saddam Hussein regime.

11 February – The Blair government deploys the British military, including armoured vehicles, at Heathrow Airport because of the apparent threat of a terrorist attack.

12 February – Five weeks before the invasion of Iraq, the Joint Intelligence Committee warns the government that the invasion of Iraq would increase the risk of terrorist attacks against the UK.

7 March – The Attorney General Lord Goldsmith sends a 13-page memo to Tony Blair warning that the invasion of Iraq could be deemed illegal without the second United Nations resolution.

17 March – In a shorter memo Attorney General Lord Goldsmith declares the proposed invasion of Iraq to be legal.

19 March – The American and British invasion of Iraq begins. Twenty-seven British service personnel die in the first 13 days of hostilities.

31 March – The US/UK Extradition Treaty is signed.

1 April – Two Algerians with ties to al-Qaeda, Brahim Benmerzouga and Baghdad Meziane, who were arrested in the UK in September 2001, are sentenced to 11 years in prison because of their involvement in terrorism fund-raising and recruitment.

1 May – President George W. Bush, from the flight deck of the aircraft carrier USS *Lincoln*, announces that 'Major combat operations in Iraq have ended. In the Battle of Iraq, the United States and our allies have prevailed.'

17 July – Scientist and WMD specialist Dr David Kelly commits suicide.

18 July – The Blair government announces an inquiry under the leadership of Lord Hutton into the circumstances surrounding the death of Dr David Kelly.

25 October – Andrew Rowe is arrested under the Terrorism Act in Dover. He is found to be carrying socks containing traces of high explosives and would be convicted of terrorism offences in September 2005.

20 November – On the day that President Bush arrives in London for a state visit, bombs explode at the British consulate and headquarters of HSBC Bank in Istanbul, Turkey. Thirty people die in the blasts and hundreds are wounded. Among the dead is Consul-General Roger Short, the top British diplomat in Istanbul.

2004

1 January – The Extradition Act 2003, including the US/UK Extradition Treaty, comes into effect.

28 January – The Hutton Report is released. It is highly critical of BBC news coverage that alleged that Downing Street had 'sexed up' a pre-war intelligence dossier while absolving the Blair government of any wrongdoing.

3 February – The Blair government announces an inquiry under the leadership of Lord Robin Butler, a career civil servant, into British intelligence surrounding Iraqi weapons of mass destruction.

11 March – Al-Qaeda-inspired terrorist train bombings in Madrid kill 191 people and injure over 2,000.

30 March – Seven men in possession of approximately half a ton of ammonium nitrate fertilizer are arrested in West Sussex as part of Operation Crevice. The Crown would later allege that they intended to bomb several targets including the Bluewater shopping centre in Kent and the Ministry of Sound nightclub in London. Five of the seven would be convicted in April 2007.

6 April – Cabinet secretary Sir Andrew Turnbull writes to John Grieve, permanent secretary at the Home Office, and notes that the Cabinet had 'recently discussed relations between the Muslim and other communities here in the UK'. The letter sets forth a number of topics related to the disaffection of British Muslims for further discussion.

19 April – Over 400 officers raid homes in the Manchester area and arrest eight men, one woman, and a 16-year-old boy. Media coverage links those arrested to plots involving attacks on Old Trafford during a Manchester United game.

10 May – John Grieve writes back to Turnbull and includes a draft of a Foreign Office and Home Office paper entitled 'Young Muslims and Extremism'.

18 May – Sir Michael Jay from the Foreign Office writes to Sir Andrew Turnbull about the findings in 'Young Muslims and Extremism'. The actual report lists a number of forces that were leading to the radicalization of young British Muslims, 'including the issue of British foreign policy, especially in the context of the Middle East Peace Process and Iraq'.

29 June – Court sentences Kamel Bourgass to life imprisonment for the murder of DC Stephen Oake.

14 July – The Butler Report is released. It is critical of the quality of British intelligence in the lead-up to the invasion of Iraq.

3 August – Fourteen men are arrested and eight eventually charged over a plot to blow up financial buildings in London. The plot's leader, Dhiren Barot, would later plead guilty and be sentenced to life in prison.

26 August – Abu Hamza, a radical Islamic cleric based in London, is arrested under Section 41 of the Terrorism Act 2000.

24 September – Four men are arrested in Brent Cross, London after they try to buy 'red mercury' in a newspaper sting. Three would be charged and later acquitted at their trial in July 2006.

19 October – Abu Hamza is charged with 16 different offences.

2 November – George Bush is re-elected President of the United States.

17 November – Tony Blair promises to bring in legislation to target the 'economic sabotage' done by animal-rights extremists.

19 November – Mohammad Sidique Khan and Shehzad Tanweer arrive in Karachi, Pakistan in order, it is believed, to attend terrorist training camps.

24 November – The government introduces the Serious Organised Crime and Police bill. It requires protesters to seek police permission before being allowed to demonstrate within one kilometre of Parliament Square. The bill receives royal assent the following April.

16 December – The Law Lords rule that the detention of nine non-Britons at Belmarsh Prison without trial, under the Anti-Terrorism, Crime and Security Act 2001, is unlawful under European human rights law, although the detentions continue.

2005

22 February – The Prevention of Terrorism bill is introduced to the House of Commons.

4 March – Hazel Blears, the minister responsible for counter-terrorism, announces in the House of Commons that 'some of our counter-terrorism powers will be disproportionately experienced by the Muslim community' since terrorists are 'falsely hiding behind Islam'.

6 March – Sir John Stevens, former head of London Metropolitan Police, warns in the *News of the World* that as many as 200 al-Qaeda-trained terrorists may be in the UK.

11 March – The Prevention of Terrorism Act 2005, designed in part to deal with the Law Lords' ruling from the previous December through a new regime of 'control orders', is given royal assent.

17 March – The Blair government announces a 'National Identity Scheme' that will see the issuance of Identity Cards.

5 May – Tony Blair and the Labour Party are re-elected in the general election.

6 July – According to the *Guardian*, the head of MI5, Dame Eliza Manningham-Buller, briefs a group of Labour MPs, assuring them that no terrorist attacks are on the horizon.

7 July – Four suicide bombers, Mohammad Sidique Khan, Shehzad Tanweer, Hasib Hussain and Jermaine Lindsay, kill 56 and wound 700 in London.

14 July – Memo from Mockbul Ali, the Foreign and Commonwealth Office's Islamic issues adviser, recommends allowing Qatari-based cleric Sheikh Yusuf al-Qaradawi into Britain because of his opposition to terrorism outside of Israel and Iraq.

15 July – Home Secretary Charles Clarke writes to the Conservative and Liberal Democrat Shadow Home Secretaries to ask for their input on anti-terrorism legislation.

18 July – The *New York Times* reports that less than a month before the 7 July bombings the Joint Terrorism Analysis Centre (JTAC) informed the Blair government that 'at present there is not a group with both the current intent and the capability to attack the U.K.' This prompted the government to reduce the threat level from 'severe defined' to 'substantial', one step above the category of 'moderate' that the Irish Republican Army was in at that time.

19 July – The *Guardian* reports that approximately 200 foreign scientists have been barred from studying at British universities in the previous four years because of a fear that they could be connected to terrorism.

21 July – Attacks by four suicide bombers on the London tube and a bus, mimicking the attacks from two weeks earlier, fail when their explosives do not detonate.

22 July – The Metropolitan Police shoot Jean Charles de Menezes, a Brazilian electrician, seven times in the head after he is mistaken for a suicide bomber.

5 August – At a Downing Street press conference, Tony Blair announces a new 12-point plan for combating terrorism.

1 September – In a video released by al-Qaeda, Mohammad Sidique Khan, the apparent ringleader of the 7 July bombings, blames British foreign policy for the attacks.

23 September – Andrew Rowe is convicted of terrorism and sentenced to 15 years in prison.

28 September – Walter Wolfgang, an 82-year-old member of the Labour Party, is removed from the Labour Party's annual conference and briefly detained under the Terrorism Act 2000 after he heckles Foreign Minister Jack Straw.

12 October – In response to the 7 July bombings, the Blair government introduces new terrorism legislation to the House. One of its measures would allow for the detention of suspects for 90 days without charge.

21 October – Police raid the homes of three men, Younes Tsouli, Waseem Mughal and Tariq al-Daour, in the London area. All three eventually face a number of charges under the Terrorism Act 2000, including inciting another individual to carry out an act of terrorism either partly or wholly outside of the United Kingdom.

9 November – Forty-nine Labour MPs join the opposition to defeat a measure contained within the new terrorism bill calling for the right to detain terrorism suspects for 90 days without charge.

15 December – The government drops the proposal made by Tony Blair at his 5 August press conference to allow the government the power to order the closure of 'a place of worship which is used as a centre for fomenting extremism'.

20 December – Abbas Boutrab, an Algerian national who used at least seven pseudonyms, is sentenced to six years in prison for downloading information on how to destroy an aeroplane with a bomb.

2006

3 February – A crowd, some chanting 'Bomb, bomb the UK', protests about cartoons published in Denmark depicting the Prophet Mohammed. At least three of the protesters, including Umran Javed, one of the protest's leaders, would eventually be convicted over their actions during the demonstration.

7 February – Abu Hamza is found guilty on 11 charges. He is sentenced to seven years in prison.

30 March – The Terrorism Act 2006 becomes law. The House forces the Blair government to accept a 28-day detention period for suspects instead of the requested 90 days.

30 March – The Identity Cards Act receives royal assent.

2 June – The Metropolitan Police raid a house in Forest Gate, London; they arrest two men, accidentally shooting one in the shoulder in the process. Both are later released without charge.

17 July – Under powers granted by the Terrorism Act 2006, Home Secretary John Reid announces that two British Islamic organizations, al-Ghurabaa and the Saved Sect, would be banned on the grounds that they had been responsible for 'glorifying terrorism'.

25 July – Three men charged with trying to acquire 'red mercury' are acquitted.

10 August – Twenty-four people around England are arrested for their involvement in an alleged plot to blow up several airliners using liquid gel explosives.

23 August – Four arrests of men accused of financing terrorism occur in Manchester over a one-month period.

1 September – Twelve men are arrested in London as part of a police operation that included the closing of the Jameah Islameah School in Sussex for three weeks.

20 September – Home Secretary John Reid is heckled by two individuals, Abu Izzadeen and Anjem Choudary, during a speech by Reid to a group of

British Muslims in London. Izzadeen is a spokesperson for al-Ghurabaa, an organization prohibited by the Blair government under the Terrorism Act 2006.

5 October – House Leader Jack Straw criticizes the wearing of the niqab, labelling it as 'a visible statement of separation and of difference'.

11 October – Communities Secretary Ruth Kelly announces that Muslim groups will receive funding on the basis that 'In future our strategy on funding and engagement must shift significantly to [Muslim] organizations taking a pro-active leadership role in tackling extremism and defending our shared values'.

6 November – Dhiren Barot receives a 40-year sentence for plotting in 2004 bombings that would have allegedly targeted the financial sector in London.

9 November – In front of an audience at Queen Mary, University of London, Eliza Manningham-Buller says that MI5 is monitoring 30 active terrorism plots and over 200 groups and networks involving 1,600 people.

2007

5 January – Umran Javed from Birmingham is convicted of inciting racial hatred and soliciting murder over his role in the February 2006 London demonstration against the Danish cartoons depicting the Prophet Mohammed.

31 January – As part of Operation Gamble, nine men are arrested in the West Midlands on terrorism charges allegedly involving the kidnapping and execution of a British Muslim soldier. Only one would be charged with kidnapping.

16 February – The Islamic Human Rights Commission releases a report examining the demonization of Muslims in the British media.

22 February – In a vote, MPs renew control orders for another year. Eighteen individuals suspected of connections to terrorism, although never having been charged with terrorism offences, are subject to such orders.

22 February – Lotfi Raissi, wrongly linked to the 11 September attacks, is denied compensation by judges for months he spent in prison after being arrested in the aftermath of 9/11.

25 February – A British government document, drawn up earlier in the

month under the title 'Extremism Threat Assessment', and distributed to MI5, Scotland Yard's Counter-Terrorist Command, the Home Office, the Cabinet Office and the Ministry of Defence, reports the *Sunday Telegraph*, warns that more than 2,000 terrorists may be plotting attacks on 'soft targets', including the transportation system, in the UK.

26 February – The Special Immigration Appeals Commission denies the appeal of Muslim preacher Abu Qatada, held in prison for much of the previous five years, allowing the Blair government to deport Qatada to his native Jordan.

5 March – The Home Office releases statistics showing that 1,126 arrests had been made under the Terrorism Act 2000 between 11 September 2001 and 31 December 2006. Of these arrests, 117 faced terrorism charges while 104 more were charged with both terrorism and criminal offences. An additional 186 faced other criminal charges while 74 were turned over to immigration officials. 652 faced no charges at all and were released. Only 40 have so far been convicted on terrorism charges while 180 were convicted on other charges and 98 are still involved in trials or facing trials.

8 March – It is announced that a career intelligence agent and specialist on al-Qaeda and al-Qaeda-related groups, Jonathan Evans, who also had experience in dealing with the Irish Republican Army, will succeed Dame Eliza Manningham-Buller as the head of MI5 when she retires at the end of March.

14 March – The Pentagon releases the transcript of the appearance at the Combatant Status Review Tribunal hearing of Khalid Sheikh Mohammed, the apparent mastermind of the attacks of 11 September 2001. Mohammed admits to his involvement in several plots including an operation aimed at destroying Heathrow, Canary Wharf and Big Ben.

22 March – Three men, Sadeer Saleem, Mohammed Shakil and Waheed Ali, are detained by police. On 5 April, they would be charged in connection with the London bombings of 7 July 2005. Specifically, they are alleged to have carried out 'reconnaissance and planning for a plot with those ultimately responsible for the bombings on the 7 July before the plan was finalised'.

24 April – Police arrest six men, five in London and one in Luton, on suspicion of inciting others to commit acts of terrorism and of raising funds to support terrorism. One of those arrested, Abu Izzadeen, had

heckled Home Office Secretary John Reid at a public event in September 2006.

24 April – Tony Blair chairs the first meeting of a new high-profile terrorism committee consisting of him, cabinet ministers, senior police officers and security chiefs. The committee, created as part of reforms to the Home Office designed to speed the flow of information related to terrorism, hears a briefing from the new head of MI5, Jonathan Evans.

27 April – The Special Immigration Appeals Commission rules in favour of two Libyan nationals, known only as DD and AS, who had appealed against their deportation to Libya. The Blair government had previously signed a Memo of Understanding (MoU) with the government of Libya to guarantee that those being deported would not face torture or other harsh treatment once returned.

30 April – In a year-long trial, a jury finds five men guilty of charges related to a plot to set off fertilizer bombs around the UK. Two are acquitted. Revealed officially in the aftermath of the verdict is that two of the 7 July bombers, Mohammad Sidique Khan and Shehzad Tanweer, were observed by British security in a meeting with Omar Khyam, the ringleader of the fertilizer plot.

6 May – A former head of the Metropolitan Police, Sir John Stevens, claims that up to 4,000 terrorists and terrorist sympathizers are in the United Kingdom.

9 May – Four individuals, including the widow of the 7 July bomber, Mohammad Sidique Khan, are arrested on suspicion of the commission, preparation or instigation of acts of terrorism, under the Terrorism Act 2000. Three of them, including Khan's widow, would be released without charge on 15 May, while the fourth would be charged under the Terrorism Act 2000 with possession of an al-Qaeda training manual.

10 May – Tony Blair announces his resignation and in a speech links the invasion of Iraq to increased terrorist attacks in its aftermath.

23 May – Police announce that three individuals, under control orders including Algerian brothers, have absconded.

25 May – Abdullah el-Faisal, a radical Muslim cleric, is deported to Jamaica. He had been previously convicted of soliciting murder and inciting racial hatred for calling on Muslims to kill non-believers.

15 June – Seven members of Dhiren Barot's gang receive sentences

ranging from 15 to 26 years in prison for their involvement in the planning of terrorist attacks.

18 June – The seventh individual subject to a control order absconds.

27 June – Tony Blair steps down; Gordon Brown becomes the new prime minister.

29 June – Police defuse two car bombs in central London.

30 June – In an attack linked to the failed car bombs, two men ram a Jeep filled with petrol and propane tanks into the front of a passenger terminal at Glasgow International Airport. One passenger receives a minor injury while the driver of the vehicle suffers severe burns that he later dies from. Over the next few days, police arrest eight people in association with the attacks, although only three are charged.

8 July – The *News of the World* publishes a map detailing the number of extremist groups or terrorist cells by region according to the Security Service. The Midlands tops the list with 80 compared to 35 in London.

9 July – A jury convicts Muktar Said Ibrahim, Hussain Osman, Ramzi Mohammed and Yassin Omar of conspiracy to murder because of their failed suicide attacks in London on 21 July 2005. All four receive minimum sentences of 40 years.

25 July – Gordon Brown officially proposes new anti-terror legislation to Parliament. Major changes include the creation of a border police force and a 56-day period to allow questioning of suspects before the laying of charges.

'An attack is highly likely.' So reads the explanation on the Home Office's website of the 'Severe' terrorism threat level that the United Kingdom is under as these words are written.[1] This is the nature of the world in the United Kingdom in the twenty-first century as the spectre of terrorism lurks in much of the public discourse. Indeed, on 30 June 2007, after a terrorist attack at Glasgow International Airport, the threat level briefly rose to 'Critical', meaning that a terrorist attack was 'imminent'.[2] This is the terrifying modern world that arrived with emphasis on 11 September 2001, the attacks that left 3,000 dead in the United States, and then came directly to the United Kingdom on 7 July 2005 with the suicide attacks that killed 56 people.

And yet, in many ways it is not a new world. Terrorism is certainly not unique, particularly in the British context. Terrorism related to Ireland dates from the nineteenth century. Nor did efforts by al-Qaeda begin on that day in September 2001. Since then, however, terrorism has been almost continually front-page news and the subject of much discussion on the airwaves and amongst politicians in the United Kingdom. The subsequent 'war on terror', so labelled by the presidential administration of George W. Bush,[3] including the invasion of Iraq, has only heightened interest in the matter.[4] With the London bombings, Britain directly became a battle zone in international terrorism and counter-terrorism, even though it had connections to these strands well before these attacks. This reality has only been heightened by the failed terrorist attacks in London on 21 July 2005, the conviction of five men for their involvement in a plot to set off fertilizer bombs in the United Kingdom, and through a series of high-profile arrests, including a number of individuals in August 2006 over an alleged plot to blow up several airliners using liquid gel explosives and in January 2007 surrounding a supposed plan to kidnap and behead a British Muslim soldier.

In the plethora of media chatter, what has been lacking since 2001, however, is a balanced, measured and informed examination of these events that offers a historical and contemporary context to what is occurring in the United Kingdom. This void applies to both studies of terrorist activity and to the response of the state, principally in the form of counter-terrorism. The writing in these areas has been dominated by journalistic accounts warning of the danger posed to Britain by terrorism, specifically of the type involving some Muslims. Then there are books documenting the threat to civil liberties by the state or the impact of the current climate on ethnic minorities. Several publications have also detailed various aspects of British foreign policy since 2001, particularly the UK's relationship with Washington.

The purpose of this study is essentially to focus on the domestic 'war on terror' by examining what has occurred in the UK in terms of terrorism and counter-terrorism since 9/11, while in turn contexualizing the period. This study seeks to answer fundamental questions: Where have we come from? Where are we now? Where are we going? It represents an effort to tie together information in the public domain in some coherent fashion in an effort to explain what is called herein the British war on terror, even though it is accepted that an actual war on terror or even terrorism is by definition unwinnable. In that sense, it will be original in the way it brings together existing material into an accessible narrative. Following on from this point is the fact that this book is aimed at a general audience. The timeline included with the book will hopefully make the events described throughout the manuscript easier to follow. The chapters that follow will also be organized in a chronological and thematic fashion. First will come a broad overview of British terrorism and counter-terrorism, pre-9/11, focusing primarily but not exclusively on the issue of Ireland. This will be followed by an examination of what occurred in Britain in terms of the Blair government's domestic security reaction after 9/11 and up to and including the events of 7 July 2005. Chapter three will offer an overview about what is known about past terrorism in the United Kingdom. A similar depiction will be made of counter-terrorism provisions since 9/11, including the drive to win the 'hearts and minds' of the so-called 'Muslim community'. A conclusion will tie everything together and speculate on what the future with the government of Prime Minister Gordon Brown might bring.

Before that, several caveats must be offered to the reader. For example, the matter of terrorism needs to be addressed. There are more than 100 possible definitions of the term. Even the British government recognizes that is not possible to arrive at a single definition.[5] Some would question whether it exists at all, arguing that it is a label applied by states against those whom they disagree with.[6] Others, including Noam Chomsky, contend that a discussion about terrorism deflects from far greater crimes committed by states that have attempted to hold a monopoly on the use of violence.[7] This author has some sympathy with Chomsky's position – states in the form of state terrorism, as opposed to state-sponsored terrorism, have killed far more innocents than all non-state terrorists have or likely ever will. Accordingly, the debate sometimes reeks with hypocrisy – in outlining his concept of a 'clash of civilizations', Samuel Huntington conveniently develops a timeline ('50 per cent of wars involving pairs of states of different religions between 1820 and 1929 were between Muslims and Christians') that emphasizes conflict between Muslims and Christians. In doing so he ignores the unprecedented death toll of World War II, including the most terrible effort at genocide in the history of humanity, that had absolutely nothing to do with Muslims.[8]

Nevertheless, this book accepts that terrorism does exist and that it involves the threat or use of violence for political reasons, such as to influence government policy, against civilians and non-combatants by non-state actors (this does not deny the existence of state terrorism but that is something separate). It also accepts that terrorism poses a real threat in the world today. The strength of that threat compared to others, such as global warming, which Tony Blair's chief scientific adviser declared to be a stronger threat than terrorism, is another matter.[9] Indeed, American academic John Mueller makes a convincing case, echoed in the UK by journalists such as Peter Oborne and Simon Jenkins, that the threat of terrorism has been exaggerated for political purposes by politicians and by private interests for financial gain.[10] There is no denying Mueller's statistical point that the risk to oneself from driving a car is far greater than it is from terrorism, or that your chances of being killed in a terrorist attack are on a par with your life being ended by an asteroid or meteorite.[11] Nevertheless, the fear generated by high losses of life due to intentional actions cannot be denied. Nor can it be denied that terrorism of all varieties has had a profound impact on British society through the enactment of a number of new laws that have restricted traditional freedoms but also through other changes. For instance, the inability to find a rubbish bin at a train station when you need one is because of terrorism. The difficulty in setting up a bank account without holding multiple forms of identification is because of terrorism. Being allowed only one carry-on and no liquids for a flight is because of terrorism. The armed fortress that is Downing Street with its heavy metal bars at its entrance guarded by armoured and armed police is because of terrorism. The examples could go on and on and on.

To deal with terrorism there needs to be a strong, unified but also a nuanced and intelligent counter-terrorism response by states. Obviously, police forces and intelligence services have a crucial part to play in this effort. But it should never be forgotten that they must function in a broader context designed by politicians. The focus of governments and institutions has to be on keeping those actively involved in terrorism small in number, and marginalized, by not over-reacting to the threat and, in the process, through repression, violence and cultural insensitivity, generating more terrorist recruits and more terrorism. Politicians have ignored this point up to the present day. The 2003 invasion of Iraq is a prime example of this. Iraq was never a central front in the battle with international Islamic terrorism before March 2003, but, thanks to the American and British governments, it is now. The toppling of the Taliban had al-Qaeda and Osama bin Laden on the run. Then came the invasion of Iraq, an event, argues al-

Qaeda expert Peter Bergen, that saved the terrorist organization: 'Without the Iraq War, their movement, under assault externally and fragmented internally, would have imploded a year or so after September 11.'[12] Indeed, the invasion of Iraq played nicely into bin Laden's efforts to portray the campaign against terrorism as a war against Islam in the form of a clash of civilizations.[13] The result has been, according to the statistical evidence, a sevenfold increase in worldwide terrorism since March 2003. Even if terrorist attacks in Iraq and Afghanistan are excluded from the survey, there has been a 33 per cent increase since the invasion.[14] The American intelligence community has recognized the significance of Iraq to global terrorism. An April 2006 National Intelligence Estimate (NIE), declassified by the Bush administration, referred to Iraq as a 'cause célèbre' for jihadists and listed Iraq as one of four key factors 'fueling the spread of the jihadist movement'.[15] The 'Iraq effect' has been felt not just there but also elsewhere, including Jordan, Spain and the United Kingdom.

Yet, the denial of the link by the British government and media supporters of the invasion continues. Often the response is to accuse those who point out the link of justifying terrorism. Demonstrating a relationship, of course, is not the same as justifying it. It is recognizing reality. Internally, those charged with investigating these issues already know this. It explains the leaks to the media by intelligence services and others from within the bureaucracy on both sides of the Atlantic, both before and after the Iraq invasion, out of disquiet about the soundness of the strategy being followed.[16] The point remains to keep terrorists, who will always exist, marginalized and on the fringes of the communities they operate in by addressing the so-called 'root causes' of terrorism, not to generate waves of recruits through ill-considered policies that do the job of Osama bin Laden for him.

Instead the emphasis by the British government and media commentators like Melanie Phillips, particularly since 7/7, has been on cultural differences, often derisively referred to as 'multiculturalism' – thus issues such as polygamy and the wearing by women of the niqab are highlighted without any effort to explain their relevance to terrorism.[17] One may dislike the niqab, but it is a choice that women have the right to make in a free society and that free society needs to demonstrate tolerance towards differences that do not affect others. Attacking Muslims for this and other cultural practices aids the cause of terrorism because it discourages integration, encourages a sense of persecution and alienation, and reinforces the perception of Islam being under attack; the exact message that terrorists wish to propagate. That no one in the Blair government thought of these implications when raising the issue of the niqab demonstrates either an ignorance to the crucial need to win 'hearts and minds' in order to achieve the long-term containment of terrorism, or that government policy is driven by crass political opportunism.

The essence of the argument that has dominated government and much of the media discourse since 9/11 is that the illiberal nature of Islamic culture is the primary cause of terrorism carried out by Muslims. Thus Muslims all over the world who are involved in terrorism – regardless of where they are, what grievances fuel their anger, what their ethnic background is, what form of Islam they practise, and how devout they are – do so because they want to impose sharia law on their societies or enslave women or destroy Christianity. The academic roots of such an argument lie with scholars such as Bernard Lewis and Samuel Huntington. The political roots are more recent and emanate from the Bush administration's response to the causes of 9/11. In his speech to Congress on 20 September 2001, President Bush made clear what had motivated 9/11: 'They hate our freedoms – our freedom of religion, our freedom of speech, our freedom to vote and assemble and disagree with each other.'[18] This view, widely popular in certain ideological quarters, has been thoroughly rejected by those with expertise in the field. Journalist James Fallows put it well in his study of the Bush administration's response to 9/11:

> There may be people who have studied, fought against, or tried to infiltrate al-Qaeda and who agree with Bush's statement [about the US being attacked because of its freedoms]. But I have never met any. The soldiers,

spies, academics, and diplomats I have interviewed are unanimous in saying that 'They hate us for who we are' is dangerous claptrap. Dangerous because it is so lazily self-justifying and self-deluding: the only thing we could possibly be doing wrong is being so excellent. Claptrap because it reflects so little knowledge of how Islamic extremism has evolved.[19]

In the same article, Fallows quotes Michael Scheuer, a past head of the Central Intelligence Agency's Osama bin Laden unit, who addressed the motivation issue directly:

There are very few people in the world who are going to kill themselves so we can't vote in the Iowa caucuses. But there's a lot of them who are willing to die because we're helping the Israelis, or because we're helping Putin against the Chechens, or because we keep oil prices low so Muslims lose money.[20]

Far from being their main selling point, the National Intelligence Estimate declassified by the Bush administration makes it clear that terrorists are hurt by 'an ultra-conservative interpretation of shari'a-based governance spanning the Muslim world [that] is unpopular with the vast majority of Muslims'.[21]

There is another element to this crucial debate that fits into an intelligent response to terrorism. Winning 'hearts and minds' is not just crucial for depriving terrorists of new recruits, something that even Prime Minister Gordon Brown has repeatedly acknowledged, it is equally essential for rooting out terrorists already in place. This comes through the generating of human intelligence (HUMINT) supplied by members of the communities where terrorists are found in the form of tip-offs or more profoundly through informers. Hostility toward Muslims through repressive measures or attacks on their culture not only drives some toward the terrorists, it encourages others to remain silent, endangering us all.

To reduce that danger will require hard work, subtlety and intelligence and, crucially, a public that is informed of the reality of the current British war on terror, including the historical context. Hopefully, the effort that follows will in some small measure contribute to a more informed debate and a better and safer future for us all.

1 The Historical Context

[T]he whole side of the wall was blown into the air. The force of the explosion was so great that three adjoining buildings were destroyed. Many persons were injured, and it is feared that some lives were lost. (*New York Times*, 14 December 1867)[1]

The explosion in London reported by the *New York Times* killed 12 and injured over 50 more. A massive bomb planted at Clerkenwell Prison by a group of Irish nationalists in an effort to free a Fenian comrade of theirs held in the prison was the cause. The explosion, which drew the withering scorn of London contemporaries at the time, including a German writer named Karl Marx, serves as a reminder that political-related violence in Britain has a long history.[2] The same point applies to counter-terrorism. The Metropolitan Police, which failed to stop the Clerkenwell plot despite receiving an advanced tip from Dublin, would eventually establish Special Branch as a lead agency to deal with the threat. Its creation occurred in the 1880s in the aftermath of a wave of Ireland-related bombings between 1883 and 1885, and because of the domestic presence of foreign radicals and revolutionaries, such as the aforementioned Marx and groups opposed to the Russian monarchy; the presence of the latter became less tenable after radicals in St Petersburg managed to blow up Tsar Alexander II in 1881.[3]

There thus exists a historical context more than a century long to the current British war on terror. This is not to say, of course, that other forms of terrorism, particularly related to Ireland, equate exactly with what is occurring in the present. Assistant Commissioner Peter Clarke, the head of Counter Terrorism Command, addressed this parallel directly in an April 2007 speech:

> Colleagues from around the world often say to me that the long experience that we have in the United Kingdom of combating a terrorist threat must have stood us in good stead. That the experience gained during some 30 years of an Irish terrorist campaign would have equipped us for the new challenges presented by Al Qaeda and its associated groups. To an extent that is true – but only to an extent. The fact is that the Irish campaign actually operated within a set of parameters that helped shape our response to it.
>
> It was essentially a domestic campaign using conventional weaponry, carried out by terrorists in tightly knit networks who were desperate to avoid capture and certainly had no wish to die. The use of warnings restricted the scale of the carnage, dreadful though it was. The warnings were cynical and often misleading, but by restricting casualties, were a factor in enabling the political process to move forward, however haltingly.[4]

And yet the two forms of terrorism are connected in many ways, not just in terms of the use of violence and what motivates the terrorists, but also in the responses, both successful and unsuccessful, of authorities toward the terrorism. Religion represents one similarity and one major difference. There was clearly a sectarian element to the conflict over Ireland that intersected with ethnicity and class, and, yet, religion was not the main motivator for those who engaged in terrorism. Religion seems more pertinent to the type of terrorism encountered by the UK since 2001, a point made by columnist Melanie Phillips in criticizing efforts by Conservative Party leader David Cameron and the government of Gordon Brown to discourage generalizations about Islamic terrorism.[5] Yet, there also appears to be an ethnic element that blends with this as those with ties to Pakistan, directly or indirectly, fuelled by grievances over Afghanistan and Kashmir, have been particularly active among the ranks of British terrorists.[6] The predominance of nationalism over religion as a motivation for terrorism fits well with the leading academic study on the topic. In his seminal work on suicide terrorism, Robert Pape demonstrates that Muslim suicide bombers come disproportionately from certain countries where issues beyond religion, principally nationalism, often in the form of resisting occupations, motivate their efforts.[7] This suggests some continuity in motivation across the centuries: the British out of Ireland and Northern Ireland; the British out of Afghanistan and Iraq.

Another obvious difference between traditional terrorism as experienced in the United Kingdom and the more modern version is suicide bombing. Terrorism related to Ireland did not involve suicide bombing nor did those carrying out attacks seek massive and indiscriminate casualties, as this was considered counterproductive to their cause. Nevertheless, as many as 3,600 people died between 1969 and 1996 as a result of violence, some of it directly in the form of terrorism, associated with the issue of Northern Ireland.[8] Before the 7 July 2005 suicide bombings, the worst individual terrorist attacks within the UK, when it came to loss of life – excluding the 1988 Pan Am 103 bombing – all involved attacks related to the issue of Northern Ireland.

Additionally, connecting the two eras of terrorism are the British state's response to them: there is not an unlimited bag of tricks when it comes to counterterrorist methods – repression, harsh interrogation methods, torture, intelligence-led policing, violence, internment, deportation, human intelligence (HUMINT), electronic surveillance, winning 'hearts and minds', losing 'hearts and minds', all apply to terrorism and counter-terrorism universally. Some important lessons about how to respond to terrorism have been gained by the British government as a result of the Ireland question; others that should have been remembered because of their significance to the post-9/11 world either were not discovered in the first place or have been forgotten with the passage of time. Chief among these is the need to win the 'hearts and minds' of a minority population in order to deprive terrorism of the host body it requires to flourish or even survive.

The Clerkenwell attack, part of several bombings in 1867 and 1868, was followed by another Ireland-related bombing campaign in Great Britain in the early 1880s in an effort to pressure the British government to grant Home Rule to Ireland. A bomb planted near a barracks in Salford in January 1881 killed a seven-year-old boy. More attacks, mainly in London, occurred between 1883 and 1885. A variety of targets were hit, including two underground trains, the offices of *The Times*, the House of Commons, the Tower of London, and even police headquarters at Scotland Yard.[9] The damage and injuries were not severe, but the attacks did lead to the formation of a special body in the Metropolitan Police in the form of the aforementioned Special Branch to track Fenians and eventually other radicals.[10]

The periodic bursts of violence continued into the twentieth century as the question of Ireland remained unsettled after centuries of brutal colonialism. The 1916 Easter Rising brought it to the fore once again and the decision by the British government to execute 16 of those involved in the ill-fated grab for independence caused far more damage to the British cause than the actual uprising. The executions alienated wide swathes of the Irish population and drove them into the arms of the nationalists. The result was a war of independence fought against the British government between 1919 and 1921 after Sinn Féin MPs elected to Westminster opted to sit in Dublin instead.[11]

In turn, this led Irish nationalists to launch attacks on the English mainland in an effort to influence British government policy toward Ireland. The Irish Republican Army (IRA), the leading nationalist organization, established units in Great Britain between 1919 and 1920. These had a great deal of autonomy and were coordinated through local Irish communities. Liverpool, for example, had between 40 and 150 active IRA men during this period. Several of them attacked the city's waterfront on 28 November 1920, damaging buildings through arson and causing hundreds of thousands of pounds' worth of damage. This initial incident was merely the warm-up for a much more audacious assault. In a remarkable example of coordination, which resembled famed Irish nationalist Michael Collins's effort that decimated British intelligence in Dublin on a single evening a week before the Liverpool attack, on 14 May 1921 the IRA conducted synchronized hits on 15 Britons who had previously served as hated auxiliary policemen in Ireland.[12] The results in London, St Albans and Liverpool were one dead, four wounded and several houses set alight.

Collectively, between the autumn of 1920 and the summer of 1921, the IRA carried out 17 shootings, 25 robberies, 294 arson attacks and 91 incidents of sabotage against telegraph lines.[13] In his impressive study of the era, Peter Hart makes a crucial point about those carrying out the attacks that has some parallel to the post-9/11 period:

> [T]his was as much a British as an Irish movement, largely composed of people who had been born or brought up in England and Scotland, or who had settled there as employed and permanent residents . . . The I.R.A. in Britain was thus a very rare phenomenon: a guerrilla movement arising from an immigrant population as part of a struggle against the host country's rule of their 'native' land.[14]

The result was widespread panic and an erratic and heavy-handed response by the British authorities. Barricades and police were deployed across central London, including around Downing Street. The House of Commons and House of Lords became off-limits to the public, and potential targets for assassination received bodyguards – two IRA gunmen had managed to kill a former Chief of the Imperial General Staff who had been born in Ireland. The government turned to security agencies that as a result of the Russian Revolution were more concerned about the threat of Bolshevism than terrorism. Gradually, British security grew more effective as efforts were centralized in London. Scotland Yard created an organized, proactive and aggressive counterterrorist response that resembled their ongoing campaign against radicalism. Human intelligence figured prominently in this equation through the use of informers and surveillance, including the opening of mail. The police also employed draconian powers, introduced by the government in London to deal with Irish nationalism. These came through two important pieces of legislation: the Restoration of Order in Ireland Act and the Emergency Powers Act (formerly the Defence of the Realm Act that had been enacted at the start of the First World War in 1914). Clause 14b of the former provided the British state with the power of deportation not just against convicted criminals but against anyone 'suspected of acting or having acted or being about to act in a manner prejudicial to the restoration or maintenance of order in Ireland'. This applied to such individuals active outside of Ireland and it supplied the government with the authority to deal with those whom it lacked sufficient evidence to lay charges against.[15] Seven men found themselves deported to Ireland from Liverpool in January 1921. Then the power was used to even greater effect in March 1923 when in a series of raids over 100 people were arrested and deported back to the fledgling Irish Free State where its government interned them. The British courts soon intervened, however. The Court of Appeal ruled Regulation 14b illegal and the House of Lords rejected a government appeal against the decision. In an even greater embarrassment, those deported were allowed to return to Great Britain and received thousands of pounds in compensation out of the public purse for the injustice that had occurred.[16]

The attacks ceased in the 1920s, but the issue of Ireland did not. Ireland had not achieved full independence and six of the eight counties of Ulster remained part of the United Kingdom in the form of Northern Ireland. This latter situation led the Irish Republican Army to decide on a bombing campaign, codenamed the 'S' Plan, in the late 1930s in an effort to force the British out of Northern Ireland, although how that would occur remained unclear even to those designing the strategy. In preparation for the conflict, IRA members in England travelled to Ireland for bomb-making training and then returned to Birmingham, Manchester, Liverpool, London and Glasgow and waited, attempting as much as possible to avoid areas such as the local Irish communities that were certain to be targeted by the security forces once hostilities began. In early January 1939, the IRA sent an ultimatum to the government of Neville Chamberlain demanding that the British leave Northern Ireland. Four days later, not having received a response, the bombings began.[17]

Explosions occurred in Birmingham, London, Manchester and Alnwick. Because the government had been unaware that the attacks were coming, the counterterrorist response took the form of increased security, the monitoring of ships from Ireland and the insertion of undercover agents into Irish communities in Britain. The attacks continued, nonetheless. In February, the IRA bombed two London tube stations. At the end of the following month, bombings took place in London followed by further explosions in three other cities the next day and seven more attacks back in London 24 hours after that. By May, the list of targets had expanded to include hotels and cinemas. Then in June, three bombs were set off in Piccadilly Circus.[18]

The British government responded with draconian anti-terrorist measures. In July 1939, after one death and more than 50 injuries due to 127 attacks since January, parliament passed the Prevention of Violence Act. Although one Labour MP had the temerity to ask in the House about possible grievances that had sparked the attacks, the Labour Party fell into line behind the Conservative government and its legislation. The Home Secretary now had the authority to issue prohibition, registration and expulsion orders, which he soon did.[19] Some 66 people would eventually be convicted of terrorism offences. Still, this did not defeat the IRA effort. What badly damaged its cause, though, was a horrific and botched attack in Coventry in which a parcel bomb abandoned by the IRA member in the wrong place exploded, killing five people in the process. The outrage over the attack led the police to search all Irish homes in Coventry. Two men would eventually go to the gallows for their part in this attack.[20] By then, with the war in Europe well under way, the IRA attacks had petered out and the counter-terrorism effort returned to a state of relaxation. The IRA re-emerged with a few attacks between 1956 and 1961, but the organization was in a moribund state by the early 1960s. MI5, however, estimated that its ranks remained as high as 3,000 members at the time of the 50th anniversary of the Easter Rising.[21]

The latter half of the 1960s would see an escalation of the conflict to a whole new level. Part of the impetus was global – the Vietnam War, the American civil rights movement and the counterculture all combined to create a more fractious world. In Northern Ireland, where the minority Catholic population had experienced decades of discrimination at the hands of the Protestant-dominated society, including the denial of employment opportunities, the resonance of the American civil rights movement appeared obvious. Campaigns to improve the lot of Catholics began in the late 1960s during a period of growing tensions. Behind the scenes was the IRA. It did not create the underlying grievances that emanated from the inequity; rather it was well positioned to reap the benefits, not just of any failure to address the grievances but equally any backlash against Catholics launched by Loyalists and their paramilitaries.[22]

Tensions and accompanying violence grew in Northern Ireland as the 1960s ended, culminating in massive rioting, with clashes between the Royal Ulster Constabulary (RUC) and Catholics in August 1969; eight died as a result of the hostilities and hundreds were injured. Although not responsible for the riots, the Provisional IRA (the IRA split over the response to the riots into the Provisional IRA, which would eventually come to dominate the field, and the Official IRA) established itself as a more radical force and sought to take advantage of the conflict by portraying itself as the defenders of the minority Catholic population.[23]

The rioting, in turn, led London to deploy the British military to ensure order in the province. Initially, many within the Catholic community welcomed this development, as the measure appeared to offer protection against attacks by Loyalists. This was due to the fact that Catholics viewed the Protestant-dominated police force of Northern Ireland, the Royal Ulster Constabulary, with mistrust. In charge of a brigade deployed in Belfast from 1970 to 1972 was General Frank Kitson, the author of a book that would become increasingly controversial because of some of the methods for dealing with insurgencies advocated within.[24] Less controversial was the soldier's belief in the need to win over the 'hearts and minds' of a population that demographically resembled those engaged in violence.[25] He additionally acknowledged the need to counter violence through intelligence in terms of collecting it, particularly through informers, analysing it and sharing it among agencies.[26]

Recognizing the desirability of winning over a populace is different from actually achieving it. In Northern Ireland, the introduction of the military further escalated tensions and, ultimately, played into the hands of the IRA, which at the time did not enjoy widespread support among the Catholic population. Soldiers, who are trained to kill, lack the sophistication of police forces in dealing with urban conflict, increasing the probability of a large-scale clash. The introduction of a curfew in 1970 and military searches of Catholic neighbourhoods, plus the occupation of 'no-go areas' in Belfast and Derry, began the process of alienation, as did the cratering of roads near the border with Ireland in an effort to stem cross-border smuggling.[27] Two other actions would prove crucial at losing 'hearts and minds'.

First, there was internment. Previously used between 1956 and 1961, it came again in 1971, with Operation Demetrius, a military operation targeted against those with alleged ties to illegal groups like the IRA. Already in February of that year, a British officer had gone on television to name leaders of the Provisional IRA in an effort to put those individuals on the defensive.[28] The operation was launched on 9 August 1971 when, at the behest of the British government, 3,000 soldiers rounded up 342 people. Missing from among the ranks of the gathered suspects, despite the existence of Loyalist paramilitaries engaged in terrorism, was even one single Protestant. This created in the minds of many the accurate conviction that the operation was fundamentally anti-Catholic. Besides the sectarian nature of the operation, it was also motivated by flawed intelligence. Some of those rounded up had previously been interned or had been active in the IRA much earlier; others seized had had nothing to do with the violence in Northern Ireland and were the victims of cases of mistaken identity – 105 were released within a couple of days of arrest, some after having been brutalized at the hands and feet of the British army.[29] The army became known for its rough interrogation techniques, the so-called 'Five Techniques', which were based on North Korean methods used against British prisoners during the Korean War. These included the use of hoods and sleep deprivation on suspects.[30]

The consensus to be found today in the literature depicting this period is that internment, which continued until 1975, was a colossal failure in the wider war against terrorism – even the Northern Ireland

Secretary at the time, Willie Whitelaw, grudgingly admitted that 'internment did nothing to stem the deterioration in the situation'.[31] The counter-terrorism disaster was a multiple one. The focus of internment on Catholics – of the 1,981 who were interned during this period, 95 per cent came from that community – ably demonstrated an apparent bias in the way security was carried out. This alienated, and in some cases even radicalized, the local population into participating in terrorism – a 1980 British study found that 60 per cent of IRA members surveyed had joined up because of the various humiliations associated with the occupation; previously, they had been uninvolved. Even if they did not become terrorists, the community's collective treatment made, not surprisingly, the supplying of essential low-level human intelligence to British security less likely.[32]

The other blow to that generation's war against terrorism occurred in a single afternoon. In what quickly became known as 'Bloody Sunday', on 30 January 1972, British paratroopers opened fire on peaceful Catholic demonstrators in Derry, killing 13 (another would die later of his wounds) and wounding 26 others. More than any other single event, this bloodshed aided IRA recruitment, as had the murder of 13 in Dublin's Croke Park by the Black and Tans, a British paramilitary force, 52 years earlier.[33] The harsh tactics of the British military had become a key recruiter for the IRA and, in that sense, distracted attention from the violence committed by the terrorist organization.[34]

That violence would soon spread to Great Britain. In a symbolic effort to strike back for the indignity of Bloody Sunday, but also to intensify pressure on the British government to withdraw from the province, the Provisional IRA launched a bombing campaign just as Irish Republicans had done in the past.[35] There was an added practical reason as well: there were 'soft targets' available across the sea from the north of Ireland. Recognizing that local Irish communities would be under surveillance, and that the police had a list of IRA sympathizers, Active Service Units, travelling under false identities, were sent from Ireland to carry out the attacks and to do so by staying clear of the usual suspects.[36] This paralleled the tactics of Soviet intelligence after World War II when its agents stayed clear of local Communists in countries such as the United States because of an awareness that they would be under heavy surveillance.[37]

The first attack, in direct retaliation for Bloody Sunday, was carried out not by the Provisional IRA but by the Official IRA on 22 February 1972. A car bomb exploded at the Aldershot barracks of the Parachute Regiment killing six civilians, including a Catholic priest. The public revulsion over the bombing prompted the Official IRA to announce a ceasefire in June of that year, turning over the field for attacks to the Provisional IRA. Their campaign started on 8 March 1972, when bombs exploded at the Old Bailey and Whitehall. Numerous bombs would explode over the next two-and-a-half years. In 1973, explosions caused injuries at two London rail stations. One on a coach on the M62 motorway in February 1974 eradicated the lives of a woman, her two children and nine soldiers. Another at the Houses of Parliament in June injured a dozen people. Then came a bombing of the Tower of London in July of the same year that killed one person and injured 41 children. The worst was yet to come. In October, seven died after explosions at pubs in Woolwich and Guildford. A month later, bombs exploded in two Birmingham pubs, less than 30 minutes apart, killing 21 and wounding 168. Advance warnings of the attacks came, but without sufficient time to evacuate the targets, one of which was located in the base of Birmingham's iconic Rotunda office building. The death toll from this last terrorist attack remained the highest for England until 7 July 2005.[38]

The attacks, particularly the final one in Birmingham, shocked Britain and pushed the Labour government of Prime Minister Harold Wilson into a dramatic response. New legislation in the form of the Prevention of Terrorism (Temporary Provisions) Act was rushed through Parliament in an all-night sitting. It defined terrorism as 'the use of violence for political ends' and 'any use of violence for the purpose of putting the public, or any section of the public in fear'.[39] Some of the powers contained within the act emanated from previous laws related to Ireland, including the 1939 Prevention of Violence Act and the Defence of the Realm Act.[40] Although in theory 'temporary' and subject to review, elements of the legislation would remain permanent. Amendments were periodically made, thus becoming technically the Prevention of Terrorism Acts. It would remain in place until the legislation was replaced by the Terrorism Act 2000 in February 2001.

The most controversial element of the Prevention of Terrorism Act allowed for the detention of those arrested in connection with terrorism for up to seven days without charge. It also permitted the government to proscribe terrorist organizations, including the IRA. Eventually a number of Loyalist and Republican organizations would be similarly sanctioned.[41] Furthermore, the new law recycled the previously used counterterrorist power of deportation. Under 'exclusion orders' the government could remove individuals suspected of terrorism from Britain and prevent their return. The Labour Home Secretary, Roy Jenkins, made no apologies for the severity of the new law: 'These powers are draconian. In combination they are unprecedented in peacetime. I believe they are fully justified to meet the clear and present danger.'[42] Five years later, a young lawyer would criticize 'exclusion orders' as unBritish in the pages of *The Spectator*: 'How is it that a country, priding itself on its tradition of civil rights, can arrange that a man is deported without even a hearing?' Then, in 1994, when the Prevention of Terrorism Acts were subject to parliamentary renewal, as Shadow Home Secretary he would attack the seven-day detention period: 'The liberty of a subject should be taken away not by the act of a politician but by a court of law.'[43] As prime minister, Tony Blair's views on such powers for dealing with terrorism would be distinctly different.

Even before the new act, the government had ratcheted up its response to domestic terrorism. The Home Secretary boasted in the House that between April 1973 and the beginning of April a year later, 1,292 individuals had been charged with terrorism offences while 1,600 weapons and 30 tons of explosives had been seized.[44] The police would eventually make arrests in relation to the pub bombings and convictions for the crimes would follow. It would later emerge, however, that the convictions had been miscarriages of justice. The cases of the 'Birmingham Six' and the 'Guildford Four' would eventually come to overshadow the horrendous crimes that they had falsely been convicted of, and again damage British efforts to combat terrorism.[45]

Nor did the new laws or police actions quell the terrorism. It grew in 1975 as a wave of attacks carried out by those actually responsible for the Guildford and Woolwich pubs, an IRA Active Service Unit that had arrived in London in August 1974, swept across the capital. The six-man squad began the attacks after an 11-day Christmas truce with a shooting on 19 January that wounded 12 at the Portman Hotel. Before the end of the month, a series of bombs would be set off, including seven in one night, aimed at London's infrastructure. After another ceasefire, the Provisional IRA attacks resumed in August with an explosion at a pub frequented by military personnel. Another 12 bombs would be planted over the next several weeks, although not all, including one targeting former Prime Minister Edward Heath, would explode. The attacks prompted Ross McWhirter, the co-founder of the *Guinness Book of Records*, to offer a reward of £50,000 for information that would aid the police in catching the terrorists – his reward from the IRA was to be murdered at his home in front of his wife on 27 November. The gang would eventually be captured through a concerted police counterterrorist effort in December after a six-day and very public standoff at a flat on Balcombe Street.[46]

Collectively, these attacks demonstrated the IRA's capability, fuelled by financial aid from the United States, conservatively estimated at $200,000 a year through the 1970s, and aided by weapons from Libya, to strike anywhere at any time. They also indicated the vulnerability of Britain to attack by hostile forces.[47] The attacks pointed to the need for a concerted, professional and coordinated counterterrorist effort to contain the wave of terrorism. Policing agencies in the form of the RUC and Special Branch dominated the field, reflecting the perception that terrorism was fundamentally a criminal activity and that during the Cold War other priorities existed for intelligence agencies.[48] Special Branch, which led the effort in Great Britain, increased their ranks from around 200 members at the end of the 1960s to 379 by

1985. Other bodies grew as well. Scotland Yard established a 'bomb squad' in the early 1970s and in 1978 this became part of what would eventually be called the Anti-Terrorist Branch.[49] The main domestic and international intelligence agencies, MI5 and MI6, would eventually develop a stronger focus on terrorism. In 1980, for example, the latter agency began to infiltrate Irish communities around Europe in what it called Operation Scream.[50] Counter-terrorism efforts received an even greater boost with the end of the Cold War when the agencies sought to justify not just the resources they received but their continued existence. After 1991, MI5, for example, began to transfer resources away from its counter-subversion and counter-espionage sections to a newly created counter-terrorism T Branch. By 1994, Britain's chief domestic intelligence agency devoted nearly half of all its resources to countering Ireland-related terrorism.[51]

Intelligence gathering would be a crucial component of such work. Electronic surveillance in the form of wiretaps and microphones was one part of this effort. British intelligence targeted the homes of suspected IRA members – planting a microphone in a physical space requires access to that space. To ensure unlimited access, an ingenious plan was developed whereby IRA members and their family 'won' free holidays to somewhere warm and sunny, thus providing unlimited access to their property for the planting of listening devices. A similar tactic would be used to recruit informers – approaches would be made to those individuals by British intelligence while the terrorists holidayed. Later, with the development of more sophisticated computers, combined with an extensive network of CCTV and roadside cameras feeding through licence registration numbers, British intelligence became able to track the movements of suspected terrorists all around Northern Ireland. Ironically, this technology would eventually come to be used across the entire UK as a means of following the movements of terrorists and non-terrorists alike; along with tracking the movement of individuals through their mobile phones, it was put to good use at the end of June 2007 when police arrested a suspect connected to a failed terrorist attack at Glasgow International Airport on the M6 motorway near Stoke-on-Trent.[52]

More important than technological intelligence, however, was the human variety. It came in an assortment of forms – from a randomly offered tip-off by someone, often on a one-time basis, to longer-term informers, either recruited from within a targeted organization or injected into it from outside. There was an important symbolism to the ability to recruit informers that spoke to the ability to win over 'hearts and minds', and thus the wider viability of a campaign against Ireland-related terrorism. 'The crucial line to be crossed is one where a passive acceptance in the Catholic community moves to a readiness to betray', was how a senior British military commander put it.[53]

Whereas terrorists could take various countermeasures to avoid electronic surveillance, it was more difficult, although not impossible, to avoid the surveillance that came in the form of a human being involved in the activity with you. Human intelligence would be crucial to the British campaign against the IRA. The latter came to recognize its vulnerability to penetration and enacted defensive tactics as a result such as moving to an organization based on cells instead of a wider hierarchy in order to reduce penetration and exposure and improve internal security.[54]

Nevertheless, in several respects informers played a crucial role in the counterterrorist effort. First, there was the obvious reason: they provided intimate details regarding operations, future plans, personnel, organization and even information on personalities, such as feuds. As 'Mike' from Special Branch told the journalist Peter Taylor: 'Sources are the lifeblood of intelligence and it all stems from there. You're fighting against a secret organization that wants to keep its secrets and you want them to impart those secrets to you. Terrorist organizations don't advertise their working parts so it's up to us to penetrate them.'[55]

Informers acting as an agent provocateur could steer the targeted organization in certain preferred directions or sabotage current and future operations. Even if informers performed none of the tasks just described they could be extremely useful by sowing dissent, suspicion and outright paranoia within the terrorist ranks – simply the awareness that informers were present affected the targeted organization and its operations. The knowledge caused the organization to look inward and view perfectly normal actions under a new and suspicious light. At its worst or best from the perspective of those engaged in counterterrorist operations, the presence or suspected presence of informers could lead to open fratricide. The IRA, which would later offer immunity to those who willingly admitted having assisted British security, killed seven or eight alleged informers ('nutting' them in IRA slang) between 1979 and 1981 (and real and imagined ones before and after this period), a number higher than IRA members killed by British authorities during the same period. It was later alleged that one of the key figures in the IRA's internal security body, nicknamed the 'nutting squad', Freddie Scappaticci, was an informer for British intelligence codenamed 'Stakeknife'. He may have participated, with the knowledge of his handlers, in the murder of other informers in order to protect his own treachery.[56]

For those recruiting informers – and one of those was Jonathan Evans, who in 2007 would become the new head of MI5 – a key aspect of their job was how to convince an individual to betray their organization, comrades and cause. Various motivations existed. Some walked in of their own accord, but these were often greeted with suspicion since their ultimate inspiration was difficult to determine.[57] For others, money was an obvious enticement but not as significant as it was in criminal investigations. Payments could be as little as £5 but rose depending on the significance and accuracy of the information supplied. Others received a weekly stipend ranging from £10 to £20 plus bonuses of several hundred pounds for strong information.[58] A number of other motivations came into play, such as the excitement of being involved in betrayal, personal grievances and grudges, disillusionment over operations that had gone badly, and compromise, often in the form of blackmail. The latter often occurred after an arrest when a deal would be offered, allowing the potential informer to avoid jail time. This became such a widely recognized practice that those released from custody immediately fell under suspicion, prompting some to admit that efforts had been made to recruit them. Coercion could take other forms. A threat to spread the word in the Republican community that an individual was serving as an informer, even if he or she had refused an offer, was an example of a particularly strong form of intimidation.[59] Sometimes the blackmail related to personal issues. Dennis Donaldson, a prominent Sinn Féin member who would later be murdered, most likely in revenge for his betrayal, said British intelligence recruited him in the 1980s 'after compromising myself during a vulnerable time in my life'.[60]

A different type of informer would emerge in the early 1980s with the so-called 'supergrasses', a term borrowed from prominent criminal cases against organized crime in Great Britain in the 1970s. These individuals were terrorists who turned against their former comrades and testified in court against them. Between 1982 and 1986, 11 of these trials occurred, leading to over 100 convictions and a cost to British taxpayers of over £1.5 million in order to resettle those doing the testifying under new identities. The practice was eventually shelved after concerns about the accuracy of the testimony being presented.[61]

The efforts against terrorism would, perhaps inevitably, slide into morally questionable areas, including the use of black propaganda and, it appears likely, the targeting of individuals for killing by Loyalist paramilitaries. In many ways, these tactics and the debate and controversy that came to surround them, and which continues into the twenty-first century, previewed the discourse that has occurred since 11 September 2001 as to what constitute acceptable counter-terrorism tactics on the part of a democratic state. The Force Research Unit (FRU), which liaised with other agencies including MI5, handled the military's informers. It would become notorious for its apparent collusion with Loyalist terrorist groups that engaged in murders, including those of two lawyers, Pat Finucane and Rosemary Nelson, targeted because of who they had represented in court.[62] Simply, the use of informers raised pertinent questions about what methods a democratic government could countenance in dealing with terrorism. Employing an informer within a terrorist organization created the real possibility that he or she would engage in criminal, even potentially violent, behaviour in an effort to establish their credibility among their comrades or to stave off any suspicion as to their ultimate loyalties.[63]

The direct use of deadly force by the state against terrorists generated further controversy. Specifically, the introduction of the Special Air Service (SAS) into the conflict led to questionable counter-terrorist operations. On 6 March 1988, most famously, members of the SAS killed three unarmed members of the IRA who were organizing an attack involving a car bomb in Gibraltar. In May of the previous year, a hail of bullets courtesy of an SAS ambush left eight members of the IRA's East Tyrone Brigade dead, one of whom was allegedly a British informer. The dead had been in the process of attacking the police station in the small Northern Irish town of Loughgall.[64]

Events like these had an impact on the IRA and its tactics, although less so on its operations in Great Britain where, perhaps fuelled by an implacable foe in the form of Margaret Thatcher, they would become more audacious. A car bomb in December 1983, for example, killed six people, including three police officers, outside Harrods department store. Thatcher's rigidity, particularly in dealing with the hunger strikers, aided the cause of the IRA as had the heavy-handed tactics of the British military in the early 1970s.[65] Her stance also made her a prime target. Even before she won the premiership, the Irish National Liberation Army (INLA) assassinated her close adviser, Airey Neave, a Conservative MP. Later, the IRA came close to murdering Thatcher and many members of her cabinet when a bomb exploded in the middle of the night at the Grand Hotel in Brighton during the October 1984 Conservative convention, killing five people.[66] These attacks hardened Thatcher's inclination not to compromise in any respect, although her government did sign the Anglo-Irish Accords in 1985. The diplomatic effort would be expanded upon by her successor, John Major, who himself faced an IRA attack when in February 1991 the organization launched three mortar shells into the back garden of No. 10 Downing Street while Major met his cabinet inside. This came less than two years after a bomb killed ten Royal Marines at their barracks in Kent.[67]

By the time of John Major's premiership, leading figures on both sides had arrived at the realization that the only solution to the problem of Northern Ireland was through diplomacy, even though some on the British side saw this as giving in to terrorism.[68] British security forces, often through the use of informers, increasingly disrupted the IRA's operations, such as attacks and weapons smuggling.[69] The RUC estimated that by the 1990s, 80 per cent of IRA operations suffered disruption in advance of their being carried out. Attacking British security forces had become particularly difficult due to a variety of countermeasures such as electronic jamming to prevent explosives from being set off. Instead, the IRA carried out several high-profile bombings in England designed primarily to cause financial damage to the British economy and, in turn, to pressure the British government into negotiating with Sinn Féin. Mortars landed on runways at Heathrow Airport in March 1994, disrupting air traffic. A ceasefire announced later in that year by the IRA was brought to an end with an enormous truck bomb that killed two people and caused considerable damage to the Canary Wharf area of London in February 1996. Four months after that attack, another huge bomb badly damaged the centre of Manchester.[70]

The potential for renewed Republican attacks remains. The Real IRA bombing at Omagh in Northern Ireland that killed 28 people on 15 August 1998, the single deadliest incident in the entire conflict, demonstrated that.[71] Periodically operations directed against the Real IRA would reach the newspapers in the era of a new and different terrorist threat but other priorities had now superseded it, as power-sharing between Sinn Féin and the Democratic Unionist Party of Ian Paisley took place in Northern Ireland in May 2007. Most have hailed this development in comparison to the violence that had gripped the province since the 1960s. Praise abounded for the roles Tony Blair and John Major had played in bringing about an end to the hostilities. Despite the arrival of peace, some prominent individuals have labelled the result as rewarding terrorism. Conservative MP Michael Gove singled out John Major for not continuing the hard line of the Thatcher period and, in a link to the supposedly meek response to al-Qaeda before 9/11, wrote that peace in Northern Ireland 'showed once again that Western nations didn't have the stomach for protracted campaigns . . . If terrorists persist, terrorism will pay off'.[72]

Regardless of such views, stability in an area once rife with sectarian and terrorist violence had arrived by the time of the new millennium. During 2000, British authorities detained only seven people under the Prevention of Terrorism Acts in connection with Ireland-related terrorism compared to 39 who were held because of international terrorism. This figure represented a decline from 12 the year before, and the lowest total since 1974.[73] As a further sign of the reduction in terrorist-related activity, the Blair government announced in 2005 that the Joint Support Group (JSG), the successor of the military's controversial Force Research Unit, would be transferred to Iraq in 2007 when MI5 would take over responsibility for security in Northern Ireland.[74] Terrorism related to Ireland had neither completely gone nor been forgotten, but a political process was now in place that offered a mechanism for addressing fundamental grievances through peaceful dialogue. In any case, the British government had more pressing concerns as more serious threats emerged. The lessons learned from more than a century of violence would both be applied and forgotten in the post-9/11 world.

2 'The Rules of the Game are Changing':[1] From 9/11 to 7/7

It was 1.46 in the afternoon in the United Kingdom on 11 September 2001 when American Airlines 11, a Boeing 767, piloted by an Egyptian engineer named Mohammed Atta, slammed into the north tower of the World Trade Center. At first no one realized what had occurred. In Florida, President George W. Bush went ahead with a visit to a school and he began, now infamously, to read to the assembled children a story called *My Pet Goat*. In Brighton Prime Minister Tony Blair was preparing to speak to the annual convention of the Trades Union Congress (TUC). Sixteen minutes and 29 seconds after the first assault, a second airliner acting like a guided missile hit the south tower of the World Trade Center live on television. There was no longer any doubt that a serious terrorist attack was under way. Less than an hour after the first plane struck its target, another jet crashed into the side of the Pentagon. One more aeroplane remained a potential missile – that threat ended when the courageous passengers on board caused the hijackers to crash it into a field in Pennsylvania almost exactly an hour after the second plane had struck. In less than 90 minutes of mayhem, 19 terrorists in an operation estimated to have cost $400,000 to $500,000 (US) had managed to kill almost 3,000 people and destroy New York City's iconic World Trade Center towers.[2] The financial damage caused by their actions would run into billions of dollars.

Shock exemplified the global reaction. Not only had the worst terrorist attack in history occurred, but also an element of it had happened live on television. Terrorism expert Brian Jenkins, writing in the 1970s, had famously described terrorism as 'theatre', arguing that terrorists generally sought 'a lot of people watching, not a lot of people dead'.[3] The events of 11 September fundamentally changed at least part of that supposed truism – the element of theatre was certainly there – the timing of the planes guaranteed that publicity would be maximized beyond any event that had ever occurred in human history. The high casualties, however, broke with most previous attacks – full jetliners had been brought down in the past by bombs on board, but there was a limit to the loss of lives in those cases from the number of passengers these could hold. The upper reach to the possible death toll in the 9/11 attacks was in the tens of thousands.

Politicians enjoyed no special immunity from the general distress. Tony Blair appeared briefly in front of the TUC audience to announce that his speech had been cancelled because of

> This mass terrorism [that] is the new evil in our world today. It is perpetrated by fanatics who are utterly indifferent to the sanctity of human life and we, the democracies of this world, are going to have to come together to fight it together and eradicate this evil completely from our world.[4]

He then travelled to London for an emergency meeting of the civil contingencies committee, officially known as 'COBRA' because the meetings occur in the well-protected Cabinet Office Briefing Room A. Special security measures for British airports and public buildings were soon enacted, most dramatically in the form of a no-fly zone over central London. In the evening the Prime Minister emerged to announce on television that what was under way was not 'a battle between the United States and terrorism, but between the free and democratic world and terrorism'.[5] It swiftly became evident that the attacks had killed not just Americans but people from 83 countries around the world, including 67 Britons, the UK suffering the second highest total after the United States.[6] This number represented the single utmost loss of British lives due to an act of terrorism. In tribute to the fallen, a three-minute moment of silence was held across the country and at a changing of the Coldstream Guards at Buckingham

Palace, the band, on the orders of Queen Elizabeth, struck up 'The Star-Spangled Banner'.

For the Blair government, hurried choices were required. When it came to foreign policy, the government made a rapid decision to align itself, in the words of the Prime Minister, 'shoulder to shoulder' with Washington. Although not the first world leader to visit the United States after the attack – French President Jacques Chirac held that title – Tony Blair sat as a guest of honour to hear President Bush address a joint session of Congress on 20 September about the attacks. During his speech Bush praised several countries for their support, including the United Kingdom, and singled out Blair in the audience with the words 'thank-you for coming, friend'.[7] Seventeen days later, American and British military forces began air and missile strikes on the forces of the Taliban and al-Qaeda in Afghanistan.

At the time, the domestic terrorism agenda seemed secondary to how the United Kingdom would respond to the al-Qaeda attack through its foreign policy. Blair's annual Labour convention speech on 2 October 2001 focused on the international dimension of what the American president had labelled as the 'war on terror' 12 days earlier. No mention was made of new domestic measures to deal with counter-terrorism, although special legislation was hastily being prepared. Before the attacks of 7 July 2005, the overriding response of the Blair government in the domestic war on terror would be through new laws. Everything else emerged from that context.[8]

There were several reasons, however, for the initial stress on the foreign response to the attacks of 11 September: the attacks had been against the United States not the United Kingdom and the origin of the attacks – at least in terms of who was ultimately responsible – seemed obvious. It was equally true that the UK had considerable experience in dealing with terrorism related to Ireland, although it had also already experienced international terrorism before 9/11.

It was the government of Prime Minister John Major that focused on the future of terrorism and counter-terrorism in the context of the increasing levels of peace in Northern Ireland and within the wider post-Cold-War world. In the mid-1990s, it appointed a panel to examine future trends in terrorism and to determine whether existing laws would be sufficient to deal with these developments. Lord Lloyd of Berwick led the 'Inquiry into Legislation against Terrorism', which issued a two-volume report in 1996. It concluded that while Ireland-related terrorism would likely continue to decline, other more global forms could be expected to increase. He recommended that the Prevention of Terrorism Act, which had been amended in 1984 to cover international terrorism, be replaced with permanent anti-terrorism legislation that reflected this changed terrorism environment and he examined potential counter-terrorist reforms within the context of the European Convention on Human Rights (ECHR). The ability to hold a suspect for one week without charge had already been found to contravene the ECHR in 1989, forcing the British government to derogate from this decision, an option allowed under the ECHR.[9]

The troublesome issue of human rights would speedily and repeatedly bedevil the desire of the government of Tony Blair to take a tougher line on non-Britons with terrorism links who resided in the UK. The matter at hand, which once again demonstrated continuity in the approach to terrorism between the pre- and post-9/11 British world, related to deportation. Four Egyptians were arrested in 1998 under the Prevention of Terrorism Act because of their alleged ties to Islamic Jihad in their home country. The government sought their deportation back to Egypt or a third country. A problem that would continue to affect the Blair government long after 9/11 soon arose: sending the men back to Egypt could lead to their torture at the hands of Egyptian security. Such moves were restricted by a 1996 European court decision that had blocked the deportation of a Sikh from Britain to India on the grounds that he might face maltreatment.[10] Despite a request by London, the Egyptian government refused to provide any guarantees with respect to the treatment of the men and the Foreign Office pointed out that even if such assurances were given it would be difficult to determine whether they had been honoured. The Blair government now faced a dilemma and the Home Secretary of the day, Jack Straw, indicated that the deportations could probably go no further. Untroubled by the human rights issues raised in the case was the Prime Minister himself. On the margins of correspondence related to the concerns over deportation, he had scrawled in his own handwriting a number of comments, including, 'This is crazy. Why can't we press on?' and 'This is a bit much. Why do we need all these things?'[11]

By then, and well before 9/11, terrorism unconnected to Ireland had become a growing concern to the British government. The Blair government would complete the path of anti-terrorism legal reform started by its Conservative predecessor by passing the Terrorism Act 2000.[12] Once enacted, it ended the Prevention of Terrorism Act, which had governed terrorism in various forms since 1974, and noticeably broadened the definition of terrorism. In that sense it fitted well with the approach of the Blair and Major governments to issues of security. Collectively these two governments had introduced several new laws, like the Criminal Justice Act 1994, the Police Act 1997, the Protection from Harassment Act 1997, and the Serious Organised Crime and Police Act 2005, which were designed to control public behaviour and restrict protest against the state and/or corporate interests. The Blair government would be, for instance, forever identified with the Anti-Social Behaviour Order (ASBO), a measure it passed into law in 2003.[13]

With the Terrorism Act 2000, there was the inclusion of an effort to 'disrupt an electronic system'. This emphasized the new technological age of the internet and that under the new law terrorism could occur without either violence or the threat of violence as a necessary requirement. The law made it clear, in addition, that for terrorism to be a criminal offence it need not occur in the United Kingdom. Most significantly, it supplied a broader definition than had previous legislation of what constituted terrorism, including a 'threat . . . for the purpose of advancing a political, religious or ideological cause'.[14]

The replacement law sparked widespread apprehension from civil libertarians particularly over the lack of a definition of what constituted a 'threat' and an 'ideological cause'.[15] The inclusion of vandalism as a terrorism offence generated the possibility for criminalizing as terrorists a whole new range of individuals. However, it also reflected concern over the emergence of new and unforeseen threats.

Home Secretary Jack Straw did little to calm the fears of civil libertarians in the aftermath of the legislation coming into law, when he was asked on BBC Radio's *Today* programme whether anti-genetically modified food protesters, some of whom destroyed such crops, could now be considered terrorists. Likely not, he replied, but added: 'if you're asking me to speculate about what kinds of groups in the end are within the definition of terrorism, I'm not going to do that. Because ultimately it's a matter for the courts.'[16]

Some aspects of the Terrorism Act 2000 were in keeping with previous British efforts against terrorism. A new version of an old power used previously against Ireland-related terrorism, for example, granted the Home Secretary the right with parliamentary approval to proscribe foreign organizations involved in terrorism. Now the government, relying on the advice of MI5 and its own lawyers, was targeting foreign organizations, some of which had a presence in the United Kingdom. On 28 February 2001, nine days after the new law came into effect, Straw issued a list of 21 such organizations (see Table 2.1) from around the world. He did so to ensure 'the United Kingdom does not become a base for international terrorists and their supporters'.[17] Most of those on the list – the choices were officially ratified by Parliament at the end of March – were involved in nationalist/separatist struggles in their home countries, the notable exception being al-Qaeda. As such, these groups posed little threat to the United Kingdom, except if they attacked British-based targets connected to their struggle back home. For them, Britain was more useful in terms of fund-raising for the struggle back home than as a site for terrorist violence.[18]

During the parliamentary debate, critics argued that the proscription feature was unfair as some of the groups being targeted operated in repressive regimes where the pursuit of one's cause through democratic means did not exist. A judge would later rule that the Terrorism Act 2000 did offer protection to tyrants and dictators from terrorism planned against them in the UK.[19] Statewatch, a civil liberties group, predicted that this shift would lead to 'the criminalisation of people granted political asylum in the UK because of the persecution which

Table 2.1: 21 Foreign Terrorist Groups Proscribed under the
Terrorism Act 2000, 28 February 2001[20]

Al-Qa'ida (Osama bin Laden was in Afghanistan at this time)

Egyptian Islamic Jihad (Egyptian group affiliated with Ayman al-Zawahiri that
would become connected with al-Qaeda)

Al-Gama'at al-Islamiya (Egyptian group)

Armed Islamic Group (GIA) (Algerian group)

Salafist Group for Call and Combat (GSPC) (Algerian group)

Babbar Khalsa (Sikh group)

International Sikh Youth Federation (Sikh group)

Harakat Mujahideen (Kashmiri independence group)

Jaish e Mohammed (Kashmiri independence group)

Lashkar e Tayyaba (Kashmiri independence group)

Liberation Tigers of Tamil Eelam (LTTE) (Sri Lankan group)

Hizballah External Security Organisation (Lebanese group)

Hamas-Izz al-Din al-Qassem Brigades (Palestinian group)

Palestinian Islamic Jihad-Shaqaqi (Palestinian group)

Abu Nidal Organisation (Palestinian group)

Islamic Army of Aden (Yemeni group)

Mujaheddin e Khalq (Iranian group based in Iraq)

Kurdistan Workers' Party (PKK) (Kurdish separatist group)

Revolutionary Peoples' Liberation Party (DHKC-P) (far-left Turkish group)

ETA (Basque separatist group)

November 17 Revolutionary Organisation (far left Greek group)

---

their membership of one of the newly-proscribed organisations
entailed'.[21] Another 21 foreign organizations, most of them Islamic,
would be added to the list of proscribed groups over the following
years (see Table 2.2).

The Terrorism Act 2000 would prove to be the bedrock legislation
for the domestic British war on terror after 9/11. The government's
initial emphasis on foreign policy and the pursuit of Osama bin Laden
and al-Qaeda in Afghanistan soon gave way to a greater focus on the

Table 2.2: Additional Foreign Terrorist Groups Proscribed under the
Terrorism Act 2000 as of June 2007[22]

Abu Sayyaf Group (Filipino Islamic group)

Al Ittihad Al Islamia (Sunni group in Somalia)

Ansar Al Islam (Sunni Iraqi group)

Ansar Al Sunna (Sunni Iraqi group)

Asbat Al-Ansar (Lebanese Islamic group)

Baluchistan Liberation Army (Baluch national group based in Eastern Pakistan)

Groupe Islamique Combattant Marocain (Moroccan Islamic group)

Harakat-Ul-Jihad-Ul-Islami (Bangladeshi Islamic group)

Harakat-Ul-Mujahideen/Alami (HuM/A) and Jundallah (Kashmiri
    Islamic groups)

Harakat Mujahideen (Kashmiri independence group)

Hezb-E Islami Gulbuddin (Afghani Islamic group)

Islamic Jihad Union (Uzbeki Islamic group)

Islamic Movement of Uzbekistan (Uzbeki Islamic group)

Jeemah Islamiyah (Islamic group based in islands of southern Pacific)

Khuddam Ul-Islam (Kul) and splinter group Jamaat Ul-Furquan
    (Kashmiri Islamic groups)

Teyre Azadiye Kurdistan (Kurdish group)

Sipah-E Sahaba Pakistan (SSP) (aka Millat-E Islami Pakistan (MIP)) and
    splinter group Lashkar-E Jhangvi (Pakistani Islamic groups)

Libyan Islamic Fighting Group (Libyan Islamic group)

---

domestic environment. Two aspects concerned the British government
more than any others: first, had there been any British involvement in
the attacks that struck the United States? Second, did the government
of the United Kingdom have laws and powers in place to deal with the
emergence of this newfangled and pressing threat? The latter was an
anxiety shared by other western governments. The United States, of
course, topped this list. Congress quickly moved to introduce and pass
the 'Uniting and Strengthening America by Providing Appropriate
Tools Required to Intercept and Obstruct Terrorism Act of 2001', more

commonly known as the Patriot Act. Three days after it was introduced, President Bush signed it into law. It provided the American government and its security agencies with a wide variety of new powers right down to checking books lent by public libraries. Canada pursued a similar path, introducing Bill C-36, the Anti-Terrorism Act, on 15 October 2001, which offered a new definition of terrorism and new powers such as the right of preventative arrest and trials in secret; it received royal assent three months later. The following spring, Australia brought in several pieces of anti-terrorism legislation that included a definition of terrorism, efforts to curtail the financing of terrorism, and power to detain suspects in terrorism-related cases for up to 48 hours for questioning without charge.[23]

The government of Tony Blair, of course, had already enacted an important anti-terrorism law less than seven months before 11 September. Nevertheless, it perceived that loopholes existed in the Terrorism Act 2000, and that the 9/11 attacks demonstrated these. Hence, as in Canada and the United States, in the autumn of 2001 it proposed a new law to respond to the threat represented by 11 September. It would come in the form of the Anti-Terrorism, Crime and Security Act 2001 (ATCSA), which the government introduced on 12 November.[24] The government stressed that the legislation was designed to address existing ambiguities in the law. The financing of terrorism, so important in terms of the pursuit of al-Qaeda, was one emphasis of ATCSA. Part 1 of the new bill replaced a section of the Terrorism Act 2000 in this area. It would also provide the police with greater power to access electronic records on individuals suspected of being tied to terrorism.[25]

The centrepiece of the proposed legislation, however, dealt with foreign nationals and paralleled the system of internment brought in to deal with Ireland-related terrorism in the early 1970s. In that sense it ignored the potential public relations damage in terms of 'hearts and minds' that such an approach could cause. It was designed to address the perceived problem that had arisen in Labour's early days when, to the annoyance of Tony Blair, the government proved unable to deport non-British individuals suspected of involvement in terrorism back to their home countries because they might face torture or other infringements of their human rights there. 'Part 4, Immigration and Asylum' allowed the Home Secretary to issue certificates against non-British individuals living in the UK were he or she to believe that 'the person's presence in the United Kingdom is a risk to national security' and suspect that 'the person is a terrorist'. In turn, this measure allowed the government to hold these individuals indefinitely without charging, trying or deporting them. This approach would be mirrored in 2002 by the United States with the creation of an internment camp at its military base at Guantanamo Bay, Cuba. There were specific reasons why the government, beyond not being able to deport the suspects, would also not charge and try them. Either the government did not have enough evidence to lay charges and seek a conventional trial under anti-terrorism legislation, or the evidence was too sensitive because it had been supplied by a foreign government, possibly through the use of torture, or else by British intelligence services that had no desire to reveal the methods and/or sources employed to collect it in the first place. Those held did have the right to appeal their certification to the Special Immigration Appeals Commission (SIAC), which had been established in 1997, and SIAC would conduct reviews of certificates. Part 4 further allowed the government to derogate from the European Convention on Human Rights in order to carry out what in effect amounted to the unlimited internment of individuals, something allowed under the Convention if there existed a 'state of public emergency threatening the life of the nation' and if the measures being introduced were 'strictly required by the exigencies of the situation'. In defending these powers during debate, Straw's successor as Home Secretary, David Blunkett, argued that the government had a stark choice between 'whether the Home Secretary should hold someone when we cannot transfer them to a safe third country, or whether we should release them into the community'.[26]

Opposition to the bill quickly emerged, both within Parliament and in the wider community. Some felt the government was rushing it through without a chance on the part of MPs to scrutinize properly the proposed law and its implications. Much of the criticism centred around what were perceived as infringements of civil liberties and human rights. In the end, it was the House of Lords, to the considerable chagrin of Blunkett, which forced last-minute changes, including refining some of the powers being granted to the police.[27]

Besides the drive to provide itself with additional anti-terrorism powers, another priority for British authorities was the possibility of a British connection to 9/11. A German link to the hijackers, particularly the ringleader of the 19, Mohammed Atta, who had lived in Hamburg, would eventually emerge. The first European arrest linked to 11 September, however, occurred in the United Kingdom. On 21 September, police raided a house in the middle of the night, arresting three people, including an Algerian flight instructor named Lotfi Raissi. Raissi had been targeted by American authorities because of tangential connections to 9/11, namely that, during a period when he was based in the USA, he had been involved in the flight training of some of the hijackers who flew the plane into the Pentagon. Raissi denied the allegations. Eventually, Washington formally required that he be extradited to face trial there. However, the terrorist suspect found himself in Belmarsh Prison where he would spend the next five months in custody as his fate was being determined. He was being being held not in connection to terrorism but officially because of previous petty crimes. Not until February 2003 would a judge make a decision in the case. He made Raissi eligible for bail and suggested that there was little substance to the American allegations. Two months later, now an embittered man, he would be released and would launch fruitless lawsuits against the British government.[28]

Another case initiated by the police, this time in October 2001, proved an equal failure. Suleyman Zainulabdin, a London chef, was arrested under the Terrorism Act 2000 and charged with 'inviting another to receive instruction or training in making or using firearms or explosives', although the government readily admitted that he had no connection to al-Qaeda. This related to a website he had established to offer instruction on the 'Islamic art of war'. In the two years that the site operated, only one person had signed up for the instruction being offered. He would be acquitted by an Old Bailey jury after four days of deliberation the following August in what was the first post-9/11 terrorism trial.[29]

A truism quickly developed with regard to many, but certainly as will be shown in subsequent chapters, not all, anti-terrorism arrests: their bark was worse than their bite. From 19 February 2001, when the Terrorism Act 2000 came into law, until 31 December 2005, 1,027 arrests were made under the law. Eight out of ten of those arrested were picked up in relation to international terrorism. Regardless of the reason for the arrest, there was only a 15 per cent chance of actually being charged with an offence. This low figure was still nearly four times higher than the chance of being charged under the old Prevention of Terrorism Act in the 1990s (see Table 2.3). The number of arrests also rose with the new legislation, although that was because of the impact of 9/11 and then 7/7 (see Figure 2.1).

Table 2.3: Arrests under Terrorism Act 2000, 2001–2005[30]

Year	Arrests	Charged under Terrorism Act	Irish terrorism	International terrorism	Domestic terrorism
2001*	131	19 (15%)	37 (28%)	92 (70%)	2 (2%)
2002	193	38 (20%)	37 (19%)	141 (73%)	15 (8%)
2003	275	47 (17%)	40 (15%)	213 (77%)	22 (8%)
2004	162	19 (12%)	16 (10%)	137 (85%)	9 (5%)
2005	266	27 (10%)	21 (8%)	237 (89%)	8 (3%)
Total	1027	150 (15%)	151 (15%)	820 (80%)	56 (5%)

Total 1990–2000 under Prevention of Terrorism Act:

	1070	45 (4%)	802 (75%)	268 (25%)	–

*19 February 2001 to 28 February 2002

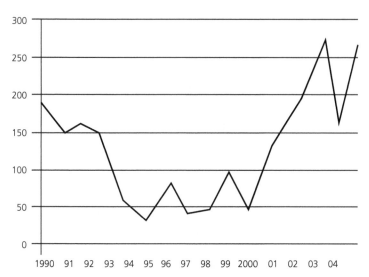

Figure 2.1: Total Arrests under the Prevention of Terrorism Act
(1 January 1990 to 18 February 2001) and Terrorism Act 2000
(19 February 2001 to 31 December 2005), 1990–2005

High-profile arrests of individuals would eventually be replaced by
the equally publicized busting of two high-profile 'plots'. A template
developed. Early morning raids ensued and suspects would be taken
away; a wave of publicity would follow, as the media vainly searched
for ties to al-Qaeda or revelations that would somehow put the
proposed attacks on a par in even a small way with 9/11. Spectacular
tabloid stories abounded, often fed by government spin doctors
seeking to generate support for the British war on terror, in terms
either of the domestic legislation or the foreign policy related to Iraq.
Often with some of the spectacular arrests there would not be any
charges, acquittals would occur, or the individuals arrested would be
found guilty on lesser charges, such as violations of the immigration
act. Left in the aftermath would be damaged lives, poisoned
community relations, and hysteria over the extent of terrorism in the
United Kingdom.

The first of the police raids on these big 'plots' occurred in January 2003. Newspaper headlines in the tabloids announced that a major plot to launch an attack on the London Underground using the poison ricin had been broken up. Police arrested six men in London on 5 January alleging that the suspects were seeking to attack the Underground with ricin in a plot that had echoes of the Japanese cult Aum Shinrikyo's sarin attack on the Tokyo subway in 1995.[31] Those arrested were North African in background, reinforcing the notion that the terrorist threat to the UK was a foreign one. Materials and recipes allegedly for making ricin were seized but, despite some initial reports and spin, there was no sign of the actual poison. Others would be arrested in the subsequent days including in Manchester on 14 January. There, one of those being arrested, Kamel Bourgass, who was living in the UK illegally, suddenly stabbed to death Detective Constable Stephen Oake. On 22 January, the Crown Prosecution Service (CPS) charged eight people with 'developing or producing a chemical weapon contrary to section one of the Criminal Law Act 1977'. In the end, however, the ricin plot did not live up to the media and government hype. A jury convicted Bourgass of the murder of Oake in June 2004, for which he received a life sentence. In April 2005, a jury also found him guilty of conspiracy to cause a public nuisance and convicted two others of possessing false passports. Four others were acquitted of conspiracy to commit murder and conspiracy to cause a public nuisance and the CPS declined to take to trial another group of suspects connected to the same case.[32]

Some openly questioned whether the government was deliberately exaggerating the threat of terrorism for political reasons, particularly to generate support for government policies like the invasion of Iraq. The ricin plot, for example, was used to great advantage by linking it to the issue of Iraq and Weapons of Mass Destruction, first by Tony Blair, who told the House on 3 February 2003 that 'Iraq is not the only country posing a risk in respect of WMD. Over the past few weeks, we have seen powerful evidence of the continuing terrorist threat: the suspected ricin plot in London and Manchester . . .'.[33] Two days later, after London apparently tipped off Washington about the arrests,

United States Secretary of State Colin Powell raised the plot again, during an address to the United Nations' Security Council about Saddam Hussein's Iraq. Powell directly connected the ricin plot to Abu Musab Al-Zarqawi, an Iraqi-based terrorist who had connections to al-Qaeda and Osama bin Laden, a point highlighted by *The Sun* in its coverage of his speech.[34] Less than a week after Powell's words, soldiers and armoured vehicles appeared overnight at Heathrow Airport. The reason for the government's sudden deployment of the troops has never been made fully clear, but it may have been connected to an admission four years later by Khalid Sheikh Mohammed in front of a military tribunal in Guantanamo Bay that al-Qaeda had planned an attack on the airport.[35]

The successor to the ricin plot was a very British terrorist plot: a plan to carry out suicide bombings at Old Trafford in the midst of a Manchester United–Liverpool football match. On 19 April 2004, over 400 police raided a number of residences in the Manchester area. Ten people, mainly Iraqi Kurds, including a woman and a 16-year-old boy, were taken into custody. Soon media fanfare openly speculated about what those arrested had been planning. *The Sun* led the sensational charge: 'A suicide bomb plot to kill thousands of soccer fans at Saturday's Manchester United–Liverpool match was dramatically foiled yesterday . . . The Islamic fanatics planned to sit all around the ground to cause maximum carnage.'[36] The discovery of ticket stubs from a Manchester United game and photos taken at Old Trafford fuelled this interpretation. As it would soon turn out, there was a more prosaic reason as to why the suspects possessed materials connected to Manchester United: they were fans of the team and had attended games in the past. All ten would later be released without charge.[37]

This perception that terrorism was being exploited for political reasons harmed police relations with the media and public and created distrust of the government.[38] The apparent politicization continued, however. The ricin plot, for example, would be used again in 2005 by Metropolitan Police Assistant Commissioner Andy Hayman, who argued in a letter in support of a 90-day detention period without charge for suspects, that an important member of the ricin plot had been released on bail and escaped. What he neglected to mention was that the police had opted to release him after only two days of detention, and not because they had run out of time for questioning.[39]

The government's exploitation of terrorism emerged in various forms. Rhetoric about hundreds of terrorists roaming the streets appeared repeatedly in the media.[40] The threat of terrorism was also deemed useful as part of a government campaign to sell the British public on the necessity of identity cards. Initially, the Blair government proclaimed that identity cards were required as a preventive tool against terrorism. The attacks in Madrid, the capital of a country with identity cards, and London, the capital of a country without them, both demonstrated that they would not have made one bit of a difference in preventing the atrocities. Former MI5 head Stella Rimington reiterated this reality in a speech in which she said that no one in the intelligence services favoured the cards. The government later dropped counter-terrorism as a justification for the card, instead choosing to portray it as a weapon against illegal immigrants.[41]

Arrest statistics appeared to support the scepticism about how serious the threat of terrorism was to Britain. In May 2002, Lord Jeffrey Rooker, a Home Office minister, offered statistics covering arrests under anti-terrorism laws. They previewed a long-term trend: the vast majority of detentions related to terrorism that occurred after 9/11 did so under the pre-9/11 Terrorism Act 2000, not the new laws brought in after that date. There were different ways of interpreting this truth. An argument could be made that the post-9/11 legislation was merely supplementary in its scope and designed to address loopholes. Equally, however, there was the suggestion that some of the legislation may have been designed to demonstrate to the public and parts of the media that the government was doing something even if what it was doing was not terribly consequential in terms of curtailing terrorism.[42] Rooker's statistics were in keeping with the numbers related to terrorism in the 1990s under the previous anti-terrorism legislation in that the majority of those detained never faced any charges (see Figure 3.2 in the next chapter). Of those eventually charged, usually it was unrelated to terrorism. The approach in that sense appeared to be 'when in doubt sweep the suspects up and sort them out later'.

Equally telling in the statistics released by the government were the numbers connected to the Anti-Terrorism, Crime and Security Act 2001.[43] The government had not waited long to deploy its new powers under Part 4 of this post-9/11 legislation. Six days after the ATCSA came into effect, the police launched raids in London, Luton and the West Midlands, and scooped up eight men. These were individuals who allegedly had connections to terrorism abroad, but not necessarily to terrorist activities within the UK. The eight would be joined by other individuals over the following months. By March 2005, 17 had been interned in total, mostly at Belmarsh Prison, which in some quarters became known as 'Britain's Guantanamo Bay', after the American prison in Cuba for so-called 'illegal enemy combatants'.[44]

Most of the men remained interned until March 2005 without charge. Their situation, and the legislation that was used to put them in prison, became increasingly problematic for the government. In July 2002, the Special Immigration Appeals Commission ruled that indefinite internment under Part 4 of the Anti-Terrorism, Crime and Security Act 2001 was both 'unlawful' and 'discriminatory', a decision that was appealed by the government. The new law also required the Home Secretary to appoint a committee to review the legislation. In 2003, that committee issued its report and singled out Part 4 for criticism, stating that it was not a 'sustainable way of addressing the terrorist suspects in the United Kingdom' and that it should be replaced. Then, in December 2004, in a case brought by some of the internees after the Court of Appeal supported the government's appeal against the SIAC decision, the Law Lords ruled eight to one against the legislation, arguing that it was incompatible with Article 5 of the European Convention on Human Rights.[45] Essentially the Law Lords decided, in the words of yet another Home Secretary, Charles Clarke, that the ATCSA was applied in a 'disproportionate and discriminatory' manner against non-British citizens whereas the government seemed to be able to deal with the British-born without such draconian measures.[46] One of the Law Lords, Lord Hoffman, bluntly suggested that the Anti-

Terrorism, Crime and Security Act represented a type of treatment that was worse than the disease: 'The real threat to the life of the nation, in the sense of a people living in accordance with its traditional laws and political values, comes not from terrorism, but from laws such as these. That is the true measure of what terrorism may achieve.'[47]

The government attempted to address the matter in early 2005 when it introduced another piece of anti-terrorism legislation. The primary purpose of the Prevention of Terrorism Act 2005 was to replace Part 4 of the Anti-Terrorism, Crime and Security Act 2001. It would do so by creating a whole new regime that could be applied equally to British subjects or non-nationals suspected of having some involvement in terrorism, thus eliminating any appearance of a double standard. These were 'control orders', which, in effect, ended Britain's Guantanamo Bay/Belmarsh Prison, replacing it with the equivalent, in a variety of forms, of house arrest. A court, when it was deemed 'necessary for purposes connected with preventing or restricting involvement by that individual in terrorism-related activity', or the Home Secretary in an emergency, subject to later approval by a court, could impose a control order. The person being selected for such a course of action had no right to see the evidence against them. Once they were targeted by the state through a control order, considerable restrictions could be placed on their life, including requiring them to wear an electronic monitoring tag, follow a curfew, report to the police daily, and live within a specified geographic area.[48] The penalty for failing to comply with a control order was up to five years in prison.

The proposed bill, admitted Charles Clarke while introducing it to Parliament in February 2005, raised 'serious and difficult issues'. These related directly to the impact of the proposed law on civil liberties since the Home Secretary would be allowed to intern not just foreign nationals but also British citizens without charge or trial. Such powers, Clarke added, were necessary to 'protect our people now and in the future. It would be the gravest dereliction of duty to wait until we have suffered a terrorist outrage here, and then respond only after the event. I am not prepared to take a risk of that kind, and I hope the

House will join me in that'.[49] Former Metropolitan Police head Sir John
Stevens echoed the Home Secretary when he argued in a newspaper
column that the delay caused by opposition to the bill provided
'comfort to the terrorists in our midst waiting to attack us'.[50] The
Prime Minister, who had once believed that '[i]f you are a terrorist you
should be under lock and key. If you are not, you shouldn't. If you are
suspected of being one, you should be under surveillance',[51] went
even further in making the case for control orders during an appearance on Radio 4's *Woman's Hour*:

> What they [the police and security services] say is that you have got to give
> us powers in between mere surveillance of these people – there are several
> hundred of them in this country who we believe are engaged in plotting or
> trying to commit terrorist acts – you have got to give us power in between
> just surveying them and being sure enough to prosecute them beyond rea-
> sonable doubt. There are people out there who are determined to destroy
> our way of life and there is no point in us being naïve about it.[52]

There was clear hyperbole to Tony Blair's contention. Control orders
would only ever apply to a handful of individuals, primarily foreign
nationals with alleged involvement in terrorism outside of the UK, not
those involved in serious domestic plotting.[53] Nor was that the only
troubling element of his argument. Implicit in his message was the
idea that in a democratic country the police and security services were
determining government policy when it came to anti-terrorism
measures.

Despite considerable opposition to the bill, including from within
the ranks of Labour MPs, the legislation was eventually passed in the
Commons and was sent to the House of Lords. There the bill ran into
serious trouble – among those voting against it was Lord Derry Irvine,
a friend of Blair's and a former Lord Chancellor – leading to a
showdown between the Lords, which would have the longest sitting
in its history over the legislation, and the Blair government. Tensions
between the two escalated because of the risk that the individuals
held in Belmarsh would be released onto the street if the new law had

not received royal assent when the old one expired on 14 March 2005. To get the required agreement for the bill to progress, it was the government that blinked first, agreeing to one key amendment demanded by the political opposition to the bill: the invocation of a 12-month sunset clause to the legislation, thus forcing parliament to review and renew it. 'Victory for the Terrorists' was how the *Daily Express* greeted the changes. Charles Clarke immediately sought control orders against the ten about to be released.[54]

The new style of internment was not without its farcical moments. The telephone number that detainees had to call on a regular basis to report on their activities did not work initially. Even if it had, one of the internees would not have been able to call since he lacked hands and had not received a special telephone that he could operate. Court challenges against the law would be launched. A May 2006 decision that the Prevention of Terrorism Act violated Article 6 of the European Convention on Human Rights was later overturned on appeal. Then there was the question of the effectiveness of control orders: over the next two years, seven of those interned would abscond, including a pair of Algerian brothers and a British citizen in May 2007.[55]

The debate over the new anti-terrorism legislation laid bare a growing antagonism toward the Blair government's domestic war on terror. Britain's foreign policy inspired much of the malaise. The March 2003 invasion of Iraq had fuelled widespread opposition in Britain. A month before the invasion, the largest protests in the history of the United Kingdom had occurred, with more than a million people filling the streets of London in opposition to any British military intervention. Even members of the intelligence community, on both sides of the Atlantic, seemed opposed to the invasion, perhaps because they realized, as leaked documents have since revealed, the dire consequences that could arise from such a course of action.[56] Once the invasion began, the opposition dissipated and, according to opinion polls, a majority of Britons, at least at the time, favoured the intervention.[57] That public support, however, would begin to fade away over time. The failure to discover any weapons of mass destruction beyond a few old chemical shells, coupled with evidence that the war had basically been planned from 9/11 onwards by the Bush administration, supported the conviction that the chief premise for the war – specifically that Iraq posed a threat to the West through its weapons of mass destruction – had either been wrong, exaggerated or outright fabricated. A report by Andrew Gilligan on the BBC *Today* programme that the Blair government had deliberately exaggerated the threat posed by Iraq in a pre-war intelligence dossier in an effort to influence political opinion led to vehement denials by the government. Furthermore, it led to the outing of Dr David Kelly, a senior government scientist, as a source for some of the BBC's reporting. Kelly subsequently committed suicide, forcing the government to appoint a commission under Lord Hutton to investigate the matter. Hutton's report, which exonerated the government while excoriating the BBC, was widely viewed as a whitewash of the government's behaviour and did nothing to quell growing public unease over the decision to invade Iraq and the subsequent war. The diminishing support at home was paralleled by events in Iraq: far from greeting the invading forces as liberators, some Iraqis actively opposed what they saw as an occupation of their land. Violence grew, as did casualties on both sides, as the situation spiralled out of control. The international image of both the United States and the United Kingdom suffered as a result, particularly with the emergence in 2004 of what amounted to trophy photos taken by American soldiers of Iraqi prisoners being abused in Baghdad's Abu Ghraib Prison. All of these factors – the overselling of Iraq as a threat, the escalation of violence with the occupation, and the apparent exaggeration of threats at home for political gain – left many in the public openly sceptical of the government by early 2005 as a general election loomed. The Mayor of London, Ken Livingstone, went so far as to state publicly in March 2005 at the time of the battle over the Prevention of Terrorism Act 2005 that 'We're more at risk from dying of bird flu than we are of being blown up by any terrorist'.[58]

Eventually bird flu may well kill more Britons than terrorism but in the short term Livingstone's comment proved inaccurate. Less than four months after he uttered the words, death and mayhem arrived in

London in the form of the worst terrorist attack in English history. The morning of 7 July 2005 was greeted by a city buoyed by news that the capital of the UK would be the host city for the 2012 Olympic Games. Tony Blair, who had performed Herculean lobbying efforts to get the Games, was particularly pleased. The Prime Minister was in Gleneagles, Scotland along with President Bush and other world leaders for the annual G8 conference.

The contrast with the mood of London by the end of 7 July could not have been any greater. For years, politicians and security officials had confidently and repeatedly warned that it was not a question of 'if' a terrorism attack would occur but 'when'. Those dire prophecies had now come true. During the morning rush hour, four young British men, Mohammad Sidique Khan, Shehzad Tanweer, Jermaine Lindsay and Hasib Hussain, ranging in age from 18 to 30, had travelled to London carrying large backpacks packed with explosives and other materials such as nails that were designed to cause as many deaths and injuries as possible. Hugging each other goodbye, they entered the tube system at King's Cross St Pancras station. At 8.50 a.m. and over the following 60 seconds the bombs carried by Khan, Tanweer and Lindsay exploded. Initial news reports referred to 'power surges' on the tube system before the truth emerged. The final bomber, Hasib Hussain, found that his targeted tube train was running late so he wandered the streets of London before climbing onto a London bus and sitting down at the back of the top deck. At 9.47 a.m. he detonated his bomb in Tavistock Square as the bus passed the British Medical Association building. In total 52 people, plus the four suicide bombers, died, and over 700 suffered injuries, many of which were serious, such as the loss of limbs.[59]

It soon emerged that the attacks had been carried out by four British citizens. Three of them were British-born and raised, while the fourth, Jermaine Lindsay, had been born in Jamaica and moved to Britain at the age of five. Then more troubling events occurred. Two weeks to the day after the 7/7 atrocity, four copycat attacks took place, three on tube trains and the fourth on a bus. Although the detonators exploded in all four cases, the bombs did not go off and no one was killed. The next day London police shot Jean Charles de Menezes, a Brazilian national on his way to work, seven times in the head because they wrongly suspected him of being a suicide bomber.

Terrorism in London sparked jitters amongst the British public and the government. Initially, after the attacks, the talk had been of coop-eration between the various political parties toward new anti-terrorism legislation. This spirit of consensus-building ended abruptly at Tony Blair's monthly press conference in August. He unexpectedly announced major new anti-terrorism proposals and took many, including his Home Secretary, Charles Clarke, who was whale-watching in the USA, by surprise. Blair's sudden intervention contra-dicted government discussion with the opposition parties over the previous weeks but seemed in tune with what was being called for by some in the right-wing press. The new proposals, which Clarke expressed concerns about privately, which former cabinet minister John Denham later called 'half-baked', and which the then heads of MI6 and MI5 failed to throw their weight behind, even gave the impression of being radically different from Blair's own previous position.[60] Earlier, he had said it was crucial to address terrorism's underlying causes, which he identified as poverty, a lack of democracy in parts of the world, and the ongoing conflict in the Middle East.[61] On 5 August 2005, 'The rules of the game are changing', the Prime Minister proclaimed. He proceeded to outline a new 12-point plan for tackling terrorism that the government would endeavour to implement over the coming year.

First, the Home Secretary today publishes new grounds for deportation and exclusion. Deportation is a decision taken by the Home Secretary under statute . . .

Secondly, as has already been stated, there will be new anti-terrorism legislation in the Autumn. This will include an offence of condoning or glorifying terrorism . . .

Thirdly, anyone who has participated in terrorism, or has anything to do with it anywhere will be automatically refused asylum in our country.

Fourth, we already have powers to strip citizenship from those individuals with British or dual nationality who act in a way that is contrary to the interests of this country. We will now consult on extending these powers, applying them to naturalised citizens engaged in extremism, and making the procedures simpler and more effective . . .

Fifth, cases such as Rashid Ramda, wanted for the Paris Metro bombings ten years ago, and who is still in the UK whilst France seeks extradition are completely unacceptable. We will begin consultation on setting a maximum time limit for all future extradition cases involving terrorism.

Sixth, we are already examining a new court procedure which would allow a pre-trial process. We will also examine whether the necessary procedure can be brought about to give us a way of meeting the police and security service request that detention, pre-charge of terrorist suspects, be significantly extended.

Seventh, for those who are British nationals and cannot be deported, we will extend the use of control orders, any breach of which can mean imprisonment.

Eight, to expand the court capacity necessary to deal with this and other related issues, the Lord Chancellor will increase the number of special judges hearing such cases.

Nine, we will proscribe Hizb ut-Tahrir and the successor organisation of Al Mujahiroun. We will also examine the grounds for proscription to widen them and put forward proposals in the new legislation.

Ten, it is now necessary in order to acquire British citizenship that people attend a citizenship ceremony, swear allegiance to this country, and have a rudimentary grasp of the English language. We will review the threshold for this to make sure it is adequate . . .

Eleven, we will consult on a new power to order closure of a place of worship which is used as a centre for fomenting extremism, and will consult with Muslim leaders in respect of those clerics who are not British citizens to draw up a list of those not suitable to preach and who will be excluded from our country in future.

Twelve, we will bring forward the proposed measures on the security of our borders with a series of countries specifically designated for biometric visas over the next year.[62]

Part of that response set out by Blair involved yet more legislation to complement the previous three anti-terrorism laws introduced since 2000: the Terrorism Act 2000, the Anti-Terrorism, Crime and Security Act 2001, and the Prevention of Terrorism Act 2005. Now joining their company was the Terrorism Act 2006, which the government introduced to the House on 12 October 2005. As with the previous two pieces of legislation, there was a reactive quality to it in that it was a response to the reality that homespun jihadists existed in the United Kingdom. The reaction was not just to the 7 July attacks or the failed attacks of 21 July. Some of the measures had been in the planning stages before this in recognition that gaps still existed in the various anti-terrorism laws.

Once again, there were several key and controversial components to the new bill. Topping the inventory was that the proposed law would allow the police to hold someone in detention without charge for up to 90 days. Opposition to the bill, both inside and outside the government, would centre on this measure. Less controversial were new offences designed to widen the legal weaponry that could be used against not so much terrorism but those who displayed some sympathy toward terrorism. First, as promised by the Prime Minister in August, there was a new offence of 'encouragement of terrorism'. This included speech or print that 'glorifies the commission or preparation (whether in the past, in the future or generally) of such acts or offences' and 'is a statement from which those members of the public could reasonably be expected to infer that what is being glorified is being glorified as conduct that should be emulated by them in existing circumstances'. Some saw this as a direct attack on freedom of speech and illustrated the danger of the new law by arguing that it would have criminalized those who had spoken out in favour of Nelson Mandela and the African National Congress's struggle against the apartheid regime of South Africa.[63]

The new bill furthermore amended the Terrorism Act 2000, by widening the criteria under which the Home Secretary could proscribe an organization. Previously, proscription required a connection to terrorism. Now, a group, even one that changed its name to avoid being targeted by the law, could be proscribed by the Home Secretary for the 'unlawful glorification of the commission or preparation whether in the past [there was no limit on how far back this could extend], in the future or generally of acts of terrorism' if it was 'associated with statements containing any such glorification'.[64] In July 2006, the government would use these grounds to proscribe two Islamic groups, al-Ghurabaa and the Saved Sect, both believed to be the successors of al-Muhajiroun, which was disbanded in 2004. It now became a criminal offence to belong to these organizations, to encourage support for them, to organize meetings on their behalf and to appear in public wearing clothes or demonstrating in some other fashion support or membership for the said groups.[65]

The government proposed other measures that targeted terrorist training and even attendance at a terrorist training camp, either within the UK or abroad. No proof was needed that the person had actually received any terrorism training. Simple attendance at a terrorism-training camp represented sufficient grounds for the committing of an offence.[66]

The most contentious amendment to the Terrorism Act 2000 remained the proposed raising of the detention period for a suspect without charge to 90 days from 14 days. The Blair government quickly leapt to the measure's defence, arguing that the complexities of modern terrorism, especially the collection of evidence, necessitated such a measure and that the police and intelligence services had requested it. This again represented a case of at best the police and intelligence services being used to sell government policy or, at worst, of their determining government policy. Left unexplored in the subsequent media coverage was why other countries also under the threat of terrorism, most noticeably the United States, did not require a similar tool. One justification for a 90-day rule not emphasized by the government was that it would allow for the extended interrogation of terrorism suspects and thus a greater likelihood of obtaining information and/or a confession.[67] The intervention of prominent police officers who openly supported the 90-day rule sparked controversy over the appearance that they were attempting to influence government policy unduly. Although the public strongly supported the 90-day rule according to some opinion polls,[68] those who counted in the debate, MPs from all parties, remained unconvinced, including 49 Labour MPs who voted against the measure. The result was the worst defeat for a sitting government since 1978 and the rejection of the 90-day rule in favour of a 28-day compromise. This represented a doubling of the previous 14 days allowed under the Terrorism Act 2000, which itself had been a doubling of the detention period without charge allowed under the 1974 Prevention of Terrorism Act. Parliament also applied a sunset clause to the new legislation that would require a review at some point in the future. Ultimately, the bill passed and came into law on 30 March 2006. The issue of the 90-day detention, however, did not disappear and continues to be resurrected again periodically, first by Blair, and then repeatedly by his successor Gordon Brown who has proposed yet more anti-terrorism legislation.[69]

All the legislation in the world, however, could not answer several fundamental questions related to the British war on terror. What had motivated the attacks of 7 July 2005? How extensive was the terrorist threat within the United Kingdom and how did the government understand it? Why was the UK a target? Did the government's approach address the cause or merely the symptoms? How effective had British counter-terrorism in the form of police and intelligence agencies been at dealing with this threat? What impact was the British war on terror having on British Muslims? And, finally, what was the most effective way to address the problem of terrorism, including its so-called 'root causes'? These questions will be taken up over the next three chapters. Tony Blair had informed the country at his 5 August 2005 press conference that 'the rules of the game are changing'. But what were the rules and what was the game?

It seemed a terrifying but momentary blip. In an era of terrorism dominated by the issue of Northern Ireland, a different form of the scourge briefly gripped the United Kingdom in the spring of 1980. At the end of April of that year, six heavily armed gunmen calling themselves members of the 'Democratic Revolutionary Movement for the Liberation of Arabistan' stormed the Iranian embassy in London on 30 April 1980, seizing 26 hostages in the process. They soon demanded the autonomy of the Iranian province of Khūzestān which bordered Iraq, and the release of 91 prisoners held in Iranian jails. When negotiations moved too slowly, the terrorists, who had been trained by the Iraqi regime of Saddam Hussein (Iraq would launch an invasion of Iran in September of that year), tied up the Iranian press attaché and executed him, dumping his corpse in the street. This triggered the beginning of the end of the siege as the government of Margaret Thatcher ordered the Special Air Service (SAS) to storm the embassy. Five of the six hostage takers were killed, but not before they murdered a hostage.[1] A new form of terrorism had arrived in the UK.

Despite this horrendous event, few could envision a future that did not involve the issue of terrorism being dominated by acts connected to Northern Ireland. That peril would slowly dissipate as a political path proved the solution to the conflict. Peace on part of that small island did not end terrorism, however. New forms would emerge and overlap with the traditional version. These fresh forms would prove particularly problematic to British authorities in the post-9/11 world since they would come to be viewed as operating outside of the terrorism norms as established while dealing with Ireland for over a century. Others would argue that the government for political reasons deliberately exaggerated the extent of the new menace since terrorism proved a useful tool for selling legislation and an invasion of Iraq. Arrests, convictions and attacks suggest that the truth lies somewhere in between. The 7 July 2005 bombings prove conclusively that the risk is potentially deadly.

But how extensive is the peril and what are its roots? Although the next few years after the Iranian embassy siege would remain relatively quiet in terms of non-Ireland-related terrorist activities in the UK, events elsewhere inevitably would have recriminations for Britain. On Christmas Day 1979, the Soviet Union invaded Afghanistan. This would lead to a brutal war lasting nearly a decade and see the launch of the largest covert operation in the history of the Central Intelligence Agency (CIA). Through Pakistani intelligence, the CIA armed the Mujahideen guerrillas fighting the Soviets.[2]

Afghanistan and the battle against communism proved not just popular with the presidential administration of Ronald Reagan but equally so with thousands of young Muslim men, who would journey to the remote country to fight the Soviets in what for many was a form of holy war. Among their ranks was a young, devout and wealthy Saudi, Osama bin Laden, a follower of a radical form of Saudi Arabian Islam called Wahhabism. He arrived in Afghanistan along with other volunteers and they were soon engaged in the life-and-death struggle against the Soviets. When Soviet troops withdrew from Afghanistan in 1989, most of the Muslim volunteers returned home, having forged links with other radicals and developed skills that would later be used against their home governments and ultimately against western countries.

These were the Afghani roots of al-Qaeda. Bin Laden himself returned to his native Saudi Arabia where he attempted to organize an Arab force to expel the Iraqi invaders of Kuwait and thus block the entrance of American troops into the kingdom. He was later expelled from his country and went into exile in Sudan. From there he eventually returned to Afghanistan. More significantly, his fledgling movement issued two fatwas in the 1990s advocating hostilities against the United States. The first was published in August 1996 under the title 'Declaration of War against the Americans Occupying the Land of the Two Holy Places'. The second, which was an outright declaration of war against the United States in particular and the West in general, appeared in 1998. This fatwa did not just advocate violence against Americans; it also singled out American allies, including, presumably, the UK, and not only military personnel or government members in these places but ordinary civilians as well: 'To kill the Americans and their allies – civilians and military – is an individual duty incumbent upon every Muslim in all countries, in order to liberate the al-Aqsa Mosque and the Holy Mosque from their grip, so that their armies leave all the territory of Islam, defeated, broken, and unable to threaten any Muslim.'[3]

The roots of terrorism connected to Asia and parts of the Islamic world were not, of course, monocausal. Equally, the forms of terrorism, be they separatist or nationalist or religious, frequently overlapped.[4] There were religious factors involving various Muslim sects, frustration at the impact of globalization on religious societies and the desire, on the part of some, to be governed in theocracies. In that sense Iran and its 1979 revolution, a country predominantly Shi'a, a minority component of Islam in relation to Sunni Islam, represented for some a triumph of the possibility of a truly Islamic state. Iran as a model of future development, however, is problematic and limited in that al-Qaeda, a Sunni organization, has a strong dislike of Shi'as. To lump together all Muslims in any respect, including the idea that there is a unitary form of terrorism connected to Islam under the label of 'Islamofascism', is grossly simplistic. It is also counterproductive in terms of developing a sophisticated response to the threat. The nature of the terrorism involving Islam often varies from place to place in response to local issues.[5] There clearly has been no 'clash of civilizations' between the West and Islam as argued by some. In fact, American sociologist Benjamin Barber argues that to make such a generalization 'is to ape the messianic rhetoric of Osama bin Laden, who has called for precisely such a war'. Presenting such a vision of the world provides al-Qaeda, which wishes to portray Muslims as under attack by western nations, with a vital recruitment tool.[6] More accurate is the suggestion that there have been clashes within Islam between moderate and more orthodox forces. However, this too is a generalization as it ignores other variables, such as ethnicity, that have relevance. Focusing solely on Islam also represents a danger to those seeking an effective response to terrorism since, as the former head of the CIA's bin Laden unit Michael Scheuer suggests, it allows those designing policy to 'take refuge in the idea that the Islamic world has gone mad, and that nothing the United States has done has caused al-Qaeda's attacks'. Then it becomes a simple case of an 'almost-crazed Muslim response to the death throes of a once glorious and worldwide Islamic civilization'.[7]

There is a spectrum of real and imagined grievances connected to the Middle East that have fuelled the rise of modern terrorism. The creation of Israel in 1948 and then, after 1967, the occupation by Israel of the West Bank, Gaza and Golan Heights has angered many in the region. So too have Israel's recent military incursions against its neighbours, including invasions of Lebanon in 1982 and 2006. On the other hand, Israel has served as a convenient scapegoat to draw attention away from the lack of freedom in many Muslim countries. There was and continues to be, for example, the repression of political movements in countries such as Egypt, the largest recipient of American aid in the world after Israel, and Saudi Arabia, a close American ally. In the case of the former, the combination of Egyptian President Anwar Sadat's signing of a peace agreement with Israel and a crackdown on Islamic fundamentalists led to his assassination in 1981. Among those rounded up in the aftermath of the murder of Sadat was an Egyptian doctor from a middle-class family, Ayman Al-Zawahiri. Released from prison later in the 1980s, he too travelled to Afghanistan where he met Osama bin Laden. Al-Zawahiri's Egyptian Islamic Jihad would join with al-Qaeda in 1998, in time for the issuing of the second major fatwa. The doctor would become second in prominence in the movement to the Saudi millionaire.[8]

By that year, the threat posed by al-Qaeda had increasingly begun to alarm the British government, particularly after the spectacular and coordinated attacks in August on the American embassies in Kenya and Tanzania that killed 225 people and wounded thousands more. At least three individuals residing in the UK, including a Saudi Arabian national named Khalid al-Fawwaz, would later be arrested by the British police in connection with the embassy attacks. The United States continues to seek the extradition of al-Fawwaz, who has admitted to having had ties to bin Laden but says that the two eventually drifted apart.[9] MI5 would come to consider a discovery in 2000 in Birmingham the first ever evidence of al-Qaeda activity in the UK. In November of that year, Bangladeshi-born Moinul Abedin was arrested in Birmingham and a cache of explosives seized. In February 2002, he would be convicted of planning to cause an explosion and be sentenced to 20 years in prison.[10]

Other 1980s events would have ramifications for the post-Cold War terrorism that gripped the UK. For the United States, the Saddam Hussein of the 1980s was Libyan leader Muammar Gaddafi, a persistent critic of American foreign policy and a supporter of international terrorism, including the Irish Republican Army. Britain had cut diplomatic relations with Libya in 1984 after a British policewoman monitoring an anti-Libyan government demonstration was killed by a burst of gunfire from the Libyan embassy. In April 1986, the Reagan administration decided to take direct action against Gaddafi. After receiving evidence of Libyan involvement in the bombing of a West Berlin disco frequented by US military personnel, the Reagan administration launched air strikes from British bases against Libya. Dozens were killed, including Gaddafi's adopted baby daughter. Libyan retaliation for the attacks came in the form of the worst terrorist incident in British history. On 21 December 1989, a bomb planted inside a piece of luggage by a Libyan agent brought down Pan Am 103, a Boeing 747 jetliner, on top of the Scottish town of Lockerbie. A total of 270 people, including 11 on the ground, died. After that, actual Middle-Eastern related acts of terrorism in the UK were relatively rare throughout the 1990s.[11]

Because these acts of violence associated with international terrorism remained sporadic, terrorism in the UK remained dominated by the issue of Northern Ireland. A gradual shift, however, began to occur in the 1990s, at least in terms of arrests related to terrorism. Detentions under the Prevention of Terrorism Act (see Figure 3.1) connected to international terrorism occurred in every year in the 1990s in Great Britain and began to outpace those related to Ireland by the end of the decade.

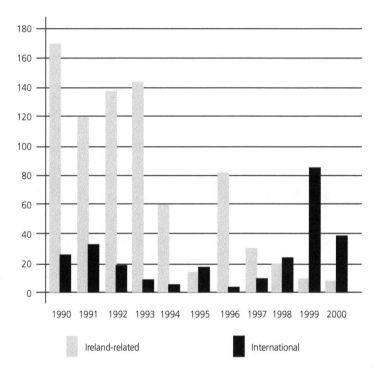

Figure 3.1: Detentions under the Prevention of Terrorism Act in Great Britain, 1 January 1990 to 18 February 2001[12]

Regardless of the type of terrorism they were detained over, most were released without charge. Of those charged, the offence more often was unrelated to terrorism (see Figure 3.2).[13]

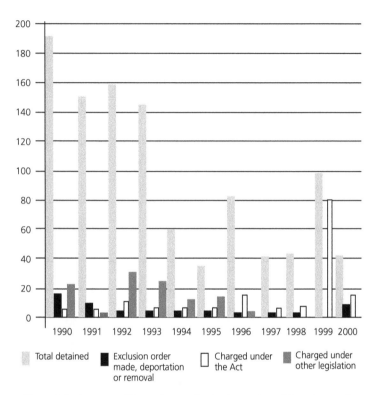

Figure 3.2: Outcome of Detentions under the Prevention of Terrorism Act in Great Britain, 1 January 1990 to 18 February 2001[14]

The 1990s and even earlier were significant for another reason: the evolution of London and the UK into a fabled safe haven of international terrorism, famously described by French intelligence as 'Londonistan'. In an important sense, although one little recognized by critics, this represented British tradition. The country had long served as a safe harbour for non-British Islamic radicals persecuted elsewhere in the world, just as it had in the nineteenth and early twentieth centuries when it had provided asylum to European radicals like Karl Marx.[15] The assistance to the former had by the mid-1990s begun to worry other nations. Frustration fuelled this perspective, and France was not the only country that expressed concern about British policies of asylum for radicals. In 1994, India's High Commissioner to the UK complained that Britons were being recruited by Islamic terrorist groups in India.[16] For the French, a main issue was that for more than ten years, the French government had unsuccessfully sought to extradite Rachid Ramda, a suspect wanted in connection with a series of Paris subway bombings in 1995 by the Armed Islamic Group, an Algerian terrorist group.[17] An anonymous European intelligence official told the *New York Times* in the immediate aftermath of 7/7 that '[t]he terrorists have come home. It is payback time for a policy that was, in my opinion, an irresponsible policy of the British government to allow these networks to flourish inside Britain'.[18]

Bob Baer, then a CIA member, observed at first hand this less publicized aspect of Britain's capital in the middle of the decade. He noticed in Arab-language bookstores the increasing proliferation of extremist literature with a strong bent against the United States. His CIA colleagues in London seemed unconcerned about the material. After all, they, unlike Baer, did not understand Arabic. Clearly, however, British freedom and liberty nurtured the appearance of materials that would not have been allowed to be sold openly in parts of the Middle East.[19] Those behind it were radicals who had arrived in the UK to escape persecution elsewhere. They came from countries with horrendous human rights records such as Egypt (Abu Hamza, who came to the UK in 1979 but periodically travelled abroad to involve himself in Muslim causes), Syria and Saudi Arabia (Omar Bakri Mohammad, who entered the UK in 1986) and Jordan (Abu Qatada Muhammad al-Massari, who arrived in 1993 using a forged United Arab Emirates passport).

These individuals would all become involved in radical and controversial religious activities through mosques, through preaching, through proselytizing, and through radical organizations like Hizb ut-Tahrir and al-Mahajiroun.[20] Omar Bakri Mohammad, for example, was initially the head of Hizb ut-Tahrir's UK branch. Then, after a falling out with the organization, he founded al-Muhajiroun in 1996; it was later disbanded and then banned by the Blair government. Al-Muhajiroun advocated

the creation of a caliphate uniting all Muslims without national bound-
aries.[21] Whilst in existence, the group's operations included involvement
at universities across the United Kingdom under a variety of names
since it was banned on some campuses. Bakri, who became notorious
across the UK when he hailed the 9/11 hijackers as the 'magnificent 19'
and the 7/7 bombers as the 'fantastic four', warned publicly in London
in December 2004 that if western foreign policy did not change the
West would experience 'a 9/11, day after day after day'. He would later
have his right to remain in the UK on an indefinite basis revoked by the
government, in part because of his association with a variety of terrorists. These included the Tel Aviv suicide bombers, Omar Sharif and Asif
Hanif, to whom Bakri admitted his connection, and several of those
convicted in May 2007 of the fertilizer bomb plot, including the plot's
ringleader Omar Khyam. In August 2005, Bakri willingly left the UK for
what amounted to exile in Lebanon and was blocked from returning by
the British government in the summer of 2006.[22]

Abu Qatada Muhammad al-Massari was another major and controversial radical Islamic figure. In the aftermath of 9/11, tapes of several
of his sermons were found in a Hamburg flat used by some of the
hijackers and he was allegedly approached for advice by Richard Reid
and Zacarias Moussaoui. Qatada himself went on the run in December
2001, apparently to avoid being seized through the internment
powers against foreign nationals contained in the Anti-Terrorism,
Crime and Security Act 2001.[23] He was discovered at a London house
ten months later and interned at Belmarsh Prison under the legislation. A judge with the Special Immigration Appeals Court (SIAC)
described the Jordanian as being 'at the centre in the UK of terrorist
activities associated with al-Qaeda. He is a truly dangerous individual.'
'Osama bin Laden's right-hand man in Europe' was the label applied
by a Spanish judge.[24] He later became the subject of a control order
under the Prevention of Terrorism Act 2005 and the government
moved decisively in 2007 toward deporting him to Jordan, a country it
had signed an agreement with guaranteeing he would not be subject
to torture or the death penalty. Jordan had long pursued him for his
alleged involvement in car bombings there.[25]

Then there was the tabloid poster boy for Islamic extremism, Abu Hamza al-Masri. Missing an eye and with hooks for hands, the former nightclub bouncer cut a striking and menacing figure and became a consistent media buffoonish hate figure. His Finsbury Park mosque was of interest to the police from at least 1999, leading finally to a raid in January 2003 in which the police discovered, in the words of one writer, a 'huge arsenal of weapons', consisting of a stun gun and handguns capable of firing blanks.[26] The litany of those who in some way were connected to Hamza and his mosque contains several names associated with modern terrorism: Richard Reid, the shoe bomber; Zacarias Moussaoui, convicted in the US in connection with the 9/11 attacks; Kamel Bourgass, who while being arrested stabbed to death a police officer; and Abu Doha, sought for extradition to the US because of his alleged involvement in a plan to bomb the Los Angeles International Airport. Hamza himself was finally arrested in 2004 after the US requested his extradition in connection with terrorism charges related to recruitment. In February 2006, a jury convicted him on 11 different charges ranging from the solicitation of murder to inciting racial hatred to the possession of a terrorist training manual. He received a seven-year prison sentence and faces the prospect of extradition to the US upon his release. During his trial he claimed that he had been reassured by the police and MI5 that he had nothing to worry about 'as long as we don't see blood in the streets'.[27]

As Abu Hamza's comment suggested, there was an implicit and possibly explicit understanding inherent in the British sanctuary offered: in return for a safe haven radicals would not organize attacks against the UK. This arrangement has, particularly since the attacks of 7 July 2005, been widely criticized as having been dangerous to the interests of the United Kingdom, as well as to other countries whose radicals found safety in the UK.[28] There is some truth in this argument, but the situation is also more complex. Having the presence of openly radical groups in London offered British intelligence the opportunity of monitoring such movements in a much easier fashion than if they went underground, one of the apparent reasons why Hizb ut-Tahrir has never been banned.[29] There was also the possibility of generating intelligence regarding trends within radical Islam. MI5, for example, allegedly tried to recruit Abu Qatada as an informer in order to 'keep terrorism off the streets of the UK' and was in contact in some form with Abu Hamza from 1997 on.[30] Regardless of the seriousness of the concept of Londonistan, it had already begun to dissolve in February 2001 with the introduction of the Terrorism Act 2000. This criminalized groups operating in the United Kingdom that were involved in any terrorist activities, be they domestic or international.[31]

It is also clear that the emphasis on 'Londonistan' obscured the possibility that instead of carrying out terrorism abroad, individuals would do so in their land of sanctuary. Nor did it embrace a scenario in which those born or bred in the UK would carry out attacks at home. This point was acknowledged by the head of Counter Terrorism Command, Peter Clarke, in April 2007:

> During the 1990s many people believed that the extremists and dissidents from overseas regimes who were active in the UK were, if anything, pursuing agendas against foreign governments, and posed little or no threat to the UK. Certainly, in 2002 the perception was that if there was a threat to the UK, its origins were overseas. The spectre of a homegrown terrorist threat was not yet with us.[32]

It was not just 'Londonistan' that helped to generate a template in which primarily the non-British posed a threat to the UK. The 9/11 attackers had not been American-born or made, as they had been with the Oklahoma City bombing in 1995. Instead, they were non-Americans who for various reasons nurtured grudges against the United States and had received al-Qaeda-sponsored training and resources in order to carry out the attacks.[33] The hijackers had all openly entered the United States by air, mainly on tourist visas. The message thus seemed clear – borders needed to be tightened and laws strengthened all for the purpose of protecting the UK against foreign terrorists seeking to carry out domestic attacks.[34] One early focus, involving some arrests, was on the presence of North Africans in the UK and their ties to terrorism. This arose in part out of the so-called 'millennium plot' in which an Algerian national was arrested as he tried to enter the United States from Canada with a car boot full of bomb-making equipment.[35] His final destination was Los Angeles International Airport. The arrest of two Algerians, Brahim Benmerzouga and Baghdad Meziane, living illegally in the UK and with ties to al-Qaeda, in September 2001 on terrorism fund-raising charges (they would later be sentenced to 11 years in prison) added to the perception of a North African threat. Due to a bloody civil war in the 1990s, Algeria had spawned its share of terrorists so such connections seemed natural.[36] Those arrested in the ricin plot were mainly North African. It, along with the Old Trafford plot that involved immigrants, further reinforced the foreign-led terrorism template. There was, however, also a protective aspect to this emphasis – the idea that British citizens, as opposed to 'foreigners', might randomly target Britons through terrorism represented a bitter and awful truth.

Other evidence began to chip away at the notion of there just being a foreign terrorist threat.[37] Already before 9/11, warning signs existed of the involvement of the British-born in terrorism, albeit outside of the UK. In 1998, Yemen arrested eight Britons, several with ties to Abu Hamza, and convicted them of involvement in a bomb plot. US missile strikes against al-Qaeda training camps in Afghanistan in the aftermath of the 1998 embassy bombings allegedly killed another young British Muslim.[38] After that, on 25 December 2000, Birmingham-born and raised Mohammed Bilal apparently murdered several people through a suicide bombing at an Indian military base in Indian Kashmir.[39]

Then arrived the post-9/11 evidence. Richard Reid symbolized the possibility of British-born jihadis striking closer to home. Born in London, Reid grew up to become a petty criminal. While in prison, he converted to Islam and, after leaving, he attended Finsbury Park Mosque where Abu Hamza offered vitriolic sermons. Reid eventually drifted around the Middle East and turned up back in Europe in the autumn of 2001. At some point, he reported his passport lost, most likely in an effort to obtain a new one that would be free of evidence of his previous travels. On 22 December 2001, he boarded an American Airlines flight to Miami. Early in the journey, he attempted to ignite explosives hidden in the base of one of his shoes in order to bring down the flight. Unable to ignite the bomb, he was quickly subdued by passengers and crew. The 'Shoe Bomber', as he quickly became known, found himself in American custody upon landing, later on trial and then in prison serving a life sentence. At the trial he confessed to being a follower of Osama bin Laden, a member of al-Qaeda, and an enemy of the United States.[40]

The example of Reid suggested that a British-born man could be radicalized enough to attempt to commit mass murder through a suicide bombing. His proposed partner in crime offered further support. Saajid Badat was as British in origin as Richard Reid. Born in Gloucester, he grew up a devout Muslim, travelling to Pakistan in 1999 where he attended a madrasa and apparently became radicalized. He soon joined the same plot as Reid, even being supplied with the identical type of shoe bomb as Reid, containing explosives from the matching batch. The difference was that he could not go through with the operation in December 2001. Instead, he disabled the bomb and left it at his parents' home where, on 27 November 2003, the police found it during a search and arrested Badat. He later received a 13-year prison sentence.[41] Finally, and perhaps most troubling of all, in April 2003, two British men, Asif Hanif from Hounslow and Omar Sharif from Derby, both with ties to Omar Bakri and al-Muhajiroun, conducted suicide operations in Israel on behalf of Hamas. The former killed three people and injured 55 others at a Tel Aviv nightclub while the explosives of the latter failed to detonate. He was found dead several days later.[42] In martyrdom videos released after the attacks, the two lamented that Muslims were being killed every day and that the real terrorists were Tony Blair, George Bush and the Israelis. The collective message of these various cases where terrorism applied outside of the UK appeared to be that by 2003, according to Peter Clarke, the head of Counter Terrorism Command, 'the UK was a net exporter of terrorism'.[43]

The government's perspective on the possibility of British citizens carrying out attacks within the UK began to evolve. In advance of the 7 July 2005 bombings, according to the parliamentary committee that investigated the matter, British security authorities had prepared for the possibility of domestic attacks by UK citizens. By 2003, for example, they had become convinced that British Muslims represented the top terrorist threat and from that year to 2005 there would be a 300 per cent increase in MI5's domestic investigative targets.[44] Eight plots within the UK, although not necessarily involving British Muslims, were allegedly foiled between 9/11 and 7/7.[45] By early 2005, then junior Home Office minister Hazel Blears publicly warned that home-grown terrorists had become a bigger threat than those from abroad.[46] She was echoing the views expressed by her boss, Home Secretary Charles Clarke. He told the House that while 'networks consisting of foreign nationals with international links remain', it was also 'clear that some British nationals are now playing a more significant role in these threats'.[47]

Already troubling signs had emerged in public in the form of arrests that would not come to trial until after the 7 July bombings had already occurred. Dhiren Barot was one example. Indian and Hindu by birth, he and his family moved to the United Kingdom in the early 1970s when he was an infant. At 20, he converted to Islam and in the mid-1990s he travelled to Pakistan. There he found his terrorist calling over the issue of Kashmir and later became connected to al-Qaeda.[48] He was one of 14 people arrested in police raids on 3 August 2004. The investigations that led to his arrest, codenamed Operation Rhyme, represented the largest counter-terrorism operation in the UK prior to 7/7. His plans, which never moved beyond the initial stages to the acquisition of materials, would have involved attacks in both the UK and the US. He confirmed his guilt when he confessed to the charge of conspiracy to commit murder in October 2006 and was sentenced to what became 30 years on appeal. Seven of those arrested with him would be convicted of a variety of charges and receive sentences ranging from 15 to 26 years in prison.[49]

Another series of arrests in 2004 against a terrorism plot would prove to be even more significant. It did so first by reiterating the threat posed by terrorism, and that part of the threat came from British citizens, and then by bringing within the domain of state security two of the 7 July bombers. Codenamed Operation Crevice, it involved another enormous effort by the police and security forces with the key assistance of an informer, Mohammed Junaid Babar, a naturalized American originally from Pakistan, with a history of being involved in al-Qaeda-connected terrorism.[50] The arrests by over 1,000 police in West Sussex of seven men, some already in possession of half a ton of ammonium nitrate fertilizer that had been secretly rendered harmless when British security switched it for an 'inert substance', occurred at the end of March 2004.[51] All would face a variety of charges, several under the Terrorism Act 2000.[52]

The leader of the plot was Omar Khyam, born and bred in Britain. Raised by his mother in Sussex after his father left when he was 11, he became involved with the al-Muhajiroun organization whilst in his late teens. At meetings, he and others would watch videos glorifying Muslim resistance against the Russians in Chechnya, and he came to believe in the need for the 'freedom of Muslim lands from occupation'. With his Pakistani heritage, however, it was Kashmir that became his personal cause célèbre. He had been on a family holiday in Pakistan as a teenager when he met members of al-Badr Mujahideen, an Islamic terrorist group dedicated to the liberation of Indian Kashmir. In January 2000, he left home to return to Pakistan and join the rebels where he received training at a camp. His family tracked him down and he was returned home but his militancy continued to grow and it would eventually focus on the UK. The tipping point for Khyam, as for many others, was British participation with the United States in invading Iraq. After this seminal event, Khyam borrowed money and travelled to Pakistan. Thanks to contacts back in the UK, there he met with Abdul Hadi, allegedly a senior al-Qaeda figure, whom the US later captured and sent to Guantanamo Bay. Khyam offered his services and became involved in what would become known as the 'fertilizer plot'.[53]

The plot needed targets. A shopping mall was a potential site. One of Khyam's conspirators was overheard on surveillance tapes suggesting they bomb the Ministry of Sound nightclub in London in part because, he said, 'No one can even turn around and say, "Oh they were innocent" – those slags dancing around.' The 29 June 2007 discovery of two cars packed with petrol, propane tanks and nails and parked near the Tiger Tiger nightclub in London led some to see a similarity in targeting and attitude between those involved in that operation and Khyam's earlier plot.[54]

Operation Crevice was a significant development in a number of respects. It showed the interconnections between some of those involved in terrorism in the UK, including two of the 7 July bombers, suggesting that the pool of real terrorists as opposed to terrorist sympathizers might be smaller than first thought. In that sense Omar Bakri's al-Muhajiroun played an important role in bringing together like-minded individuals and creating the environment that would allow for finding new recruits. The clear tie to Pakistan of British terrorism was also on display. This particularly applied to Kashmir as a source of grievance to go with all of the other grievances involving Muslims.[55] Finally, the convictions by a jury of some of those connected to the plot represented the first successful conclusion from the perspective of the government of a mass-arrest plan and went some way to restoring confidence after the Old Trafford and ricin debacles. Still, other implications for the future remained. Getting the convictions had been no easy matter. The trial covered 13 months and the jury took 27 days, the longest deliberation in British criminal trial history, to convict Khyam and four other men while acquitting two others.[56]

Because of the complicated nature of Operation Crevice and the lengthy trial, the arrests actually occurred before the bombings of 7 July and then finished well after reports into 7/7 had emerged. To ensure proper legal procedures, some details were suppressed until the conclusion of the trial. One bit of information released was surveillance materials. It quickly emerged that two of the 7 July bombers, including the apparent ringleader of the operation, Mohammad Sidique Khan, had been in contact with Omar Khyam and some of the others involved in the fertilizer plot, having turned up four separate times in MI5's surveillance. The contact demonstrated the possibility of overlapping cells with common linkages between them and the centrally important role played by al-Muhajiroun and others in bringing together like-minded individuals.[57] In that sense, according to the BBC, those involved with the fertilizer and 7 July plots represented more traditional terrorism in the form of 'tight cells of Jihadi activists swimming in a sea of like-minded individuals' and not self-radicalized individuals randomly drawn to terrorism through the internet.[58]

While the fertilizer plot marked several terrorism firsts, it was surpassed in terms of significance by the 7 July 2005 bombings carried out by Mohammad Sidique Khan, Shehzad Tanweer, Hasib Hussain and Jermaine Lindsay. They were the first suicide bombings carried out in the history of the United Kingdom, and they were carried out by British citizens. That truth seemed difficult for some to grasp. Initial media speculation and even the British government itself focused on the possibility of a North African angle, a legacy of the apparent pattern to international terrorism since 9/11.[59]

Beyond those facts, there was a clear pattern to what the bombers did that fits with some of the other arrests, convictions and types of terrorism active in the UK in the post-9/11 period. Khan and Tanweer travelled to Pakistan in November 2004 for training for the operation, although the extent of this and how much direct control was exerted over their operation by al-Qaeda or al-Qaeda-affiliated groups remains unknown. While in Pakistan the two of them made martyrdom videos. It was also in the lead-up to the attacks that both Khan and Tanweer turned up in surveillance videos and recordings of some of those involved with the fertilizer plot. In the end, MI5 decided they were not a serious threat in relation to others whom they maintained surveillance against.[60] Then for the four it was a case of assembling the necessary materials readily available over the counter, and building the bombs. Warning signs noticed by the men's families, like bleached hair due to chemicals, was put down to swimming in a pool with a strong chlorine content. Backpacks were bought and a reconnaissance trip made by three of the bombers to London. On 7 July, in the midst of the G8 Summit in Scotland, the three from Leeds drove to Luton where Jermaine Lindsay joined them. Then it was on to London and death for them and 52 others. The backpack bombs cost only a few hundred pounds and the instructions on how to build them were readily available over the internet.[61]

As with the Barot case and the fertilizer plot, there was a single key individual behind the 7 July atrocities. Working as a teaching assistant, Mohammad Sidique Khan appeared to be a model citizen. His involvement in helping local Muslim youths outside of school put him in an important position to recruit young and impressionable men, including two of the other bombers. Khan, himself, had been drawn to radical Islamic politics in the late 1990s. A detailed study of his life found a complicated explanation as to his motivations that interconnected religion and ethnicity. Like the children of many immigrants, he grappled with being a second-generation British Asian, finding himself in some ways not at home in either milieu. The cultural conflict grew as he resisted pressure to marry a bride selected by his family and instead married a non-Pakistani woman he had met while at university. The Wahhabi version of Islam that he was drawn to offered him a respite from his family's more traditional Islam; it allowed for its adherents to choose their own spouses and provided a religious identity to call their own that was unconnected to either Britain or Pakistan.[62] It was that radical version of Islam that brought Khan into terrorism, although this still did not offer a complete explanation as to why he and his companions decided to kill themselves and others.

In the aftermath of 7/7, the Blair government initially displayed a willingness to reflect and consider the best course to follow instead of lashing out wildly. Blair himself pointed to political grievances connected to the Middle East as a cause of terrorism and something that needed to be addressed. He further admitted at a 26 July 2005 press conference that issues such as Iraq could be used to 'recruit' terrorists.[63] In these responses, the government reflected the repeated advice it had been receiving internally since before the bombings, namely that a key factor in the radicalization of young British Muslims was foreign policy, particularly British involvement alongside the United States in Iraq.

Two separate issues were at work here, although public commentary often failed to separate them. First, there was the question of how young British Muslims were being recruited into terrorism. This was the category that ultimately the Blair government and others would focus on. At his 5 August 2005 press conference, the Prime Minister, to the surprise of his colleagues and opposition parties, set out 12 steps that concentrated on the how: proscribing organizations, ending the glorification of terrorism, closing mosques, deporting radicals, etc. In that sense, the Blair approach found echoes from elsewhere in the UK. A study, to widespread publicity, blamed British universities for allowing 'access to extreme terror-justifying ideas'.[64] Even if there was greater evidence for the culpability of universities than had been presented so far, it still did not explain why young people signed up to a terrorist cause and were prepared to lay down their lives. The picture was not simple. Omar Sheikh, who killed Daniel Pearl, was involved in the Islamic Society at the London School of Economics in the early 1990s, thus fitting the supposed connection between universities and terrorism. What drew him into terrorism, however, was not attendance at a university but the treatment of Bosnian Muslims.[65] Terrorists like Sheikh could be drawn into radicalism anywhere and have been in prisons, mosques, youth clubs, Pakistan and other environs, including, as arrests in June and July 2007 after failed attacks in London and Glasgow suggested, the National Health Service.[66] In the future an increasing concern for intelligence services will not be the recruitment of youth into a path of violence at public and open institutions like universities, where there can be scrutiny and monitoring; it will be the conscription of young people into terrorism in the privacy and anonymity of their computer and bedroom.[67]

The second and less examined aspect is the more difficult one to comprehend: why would young British Muslims become involved in terrorism? Any single explanation by definition is too simplistic. Instead, a multitude of important points are relevant: religion, immigration, familial and generational relations, ethnicity, racism, youth and, of course, British and western policies, including foreign policy in the Middle East and south and central Asia.

That, of course, was not how the government officially understood the motivation of the terrorists. Charles Clarke, at the time the Home Secretary, gave some indication of its thinking, at least as part of the Blair post-5 August 2005 press conference approach. He did so when he gave a speech about terrorism in front of the Heritage Foundation, a conservative Washington think-tank with ties to the neoconservative movement:

[T]he threat we face is ideological. It is not driven by poverty, or by social exclusion, or by racial hatred . . . It is equally wrong to claim, as some do, that the motivation of AQ [al-Qaeda] and their allies is driven by some desire to seek justice in the Middle East – the part of the world where progress has been most difficult to achieve in the past 30 years . . . In fact the whole approach of AQ and their like is more akin to 19th-century nihilism than to 20th-century liberation.[68]

Clarke's, or more accurately, his speechwriters' interpretations of terrorism were problematic in several respects. First, they reflected a simplistic view of al-Qaeda's motivation that President Bush had intro-duced in September 2001 ('they hate us because we are free') that had been widely repudiated.[69] Second, they displayed a fundamental lack of reflection as to why someone would willingly blow himself and others up.

It was a second speech by yet another Blair cabinet minister that displayed decidedly different thinking and at least in part a growing recognition that the place of foreign policy as a 'root cause' of terrorism could not be ignored. Then International Development Secretary Hilary Benn received considerable media coverage for the first part of his speech when he argued that the phrase 'war on terror' was counterproductive, in that it lumped together a wide range of groups and interests under a single terrorist threat.[70] Largely ignored by the media was the part of Benn's speech that addressed the moti-vation of terrorists like the 7/7 bombers:

I asked myself – the community asked itself – how could British people do this to their neighbours? What was it about these young men that led them to nurture such hatred in their midst? And while we try hard to understand what we cannot forgive and should not forgive is their criminal acts of murder.

Many British Muslims – and non-Muslims – are angry about Iraq, angry about the failure to make peace in the Middle East, others are angry about what they see as other historical injustices in the wider world . . . And what we can surely all agree on is that we have to do something about injustice. That is why the Middle East Peace Process is such a priority for us, because a peaceful Palestine living alongside a peaceful Israel would not just help that region, but it would transform the politics of the whole world. That is why we have to fight poverty across the world.

Now that won't stop all the extremists – there are some for whom ideological purity is reason enough to justify mass murder. But it will rob them of their cloak, their claim to legitimacy, and show them for what they are – capable of destruction, but incapable of building a better future.[71]

Benn was acknowledging the obvious – that whereas the hardcore leaders of al-Qaeda and its various outlet groups might be motivated by ideology in the form of religious fanaticism, many of those whom they recruited chose to join up for other reasons, including out of a sense of injustice. The path followed by British foreign policy after 9/11 only intensified such motivations. This was the elephant in the room that neither the Blair government nor the cheerleaders for the American war on terror, in particular those who advocated the invasion of Iraq, would address.

Repeated vehement denials on the government's part cannot counter the body of evidence that has emerged since the invasion of Iraq as to the significance (although not exclusively so) of foreign policy as a motivation of terrorism. First, there were the words of the suicide bombers themselves. Mohammad Sidique Khan's video appeared on Al Jazeera at the end of August 2005 and contained the following description of his motivation for his murderous suicide attack:

Your democratically elected governments continuously perpetuate atrocities against my people all over the world. And your support of them makes you directly responsible, just as I am directly responsible for protecting and avenging my Muslim brothers and sisters.

Until we feel security, you will be our targets. And until you stop the bombing, gassing, imprisonment and torture of my people we will not stop this fight.

We are at war and I am a soldier. Now you too will taste the reality of this situation.[72]

These themes were reiterated by Tanweer in his martyrdom video that appeared on Al Jazeera just before the first anniversary of the 7/7 bombings:

To the non-Muslims of Britain, you may wonder what you have done to deserve this. You are those who have voted in your government, who in turn have, and still continue to this day, continue to oppress our mothers, children, brothers and sisters, from the east to the west, in Palestine, Afghanistan, Iraq, and Chechnya. Your government has openly supported the genocide of over 150,000 innocent Muslims in Falluja.[73]

Then there was the internal evidence produced by government agencies, and ignored by their political masters both before and after the invasion of Iraq, which has leaked out in dribs and drabs. In January 2003, the CIA, Britain's chief foreign intelligence partner, told the Bush administration that invading Iraq could embolden al-Qaeda and Iran and lead to chaos. The following month, the Joint Intelligence Committee (JIC), reflecting the collective view of the British intelligence community, warned the Blair government that 'al-Qa'eda and associated groups continued to represent by far the greatest terrorist threat to Western interests, and that threat would be heightened by military action against Iraq'.[74] A 2004 joint Foreign Office/Home Office report, entitled 'Young Muslims and Extremism', aimed at examining the radicalization of British Muslim youth, addressed directly the issue of foreign policy and its significance in the post-9/11 environment:

It seems that a particularly strong cause of disillusionment amongst Muslims including young Muslims is a perceived 'double standard' in the foreign policy of western governments (and often those of Muslim governments), in particular Britain and the US . . .

Perceived Western bias in Israel's favour over the Israel/Palestinian conflict is a key long term grievance of the international Muslim community which probably influences British Muslims.

This perception seems to have become more acute post 9/11. The perception is that passive 'oppression', as demonstrated in British foreign policy, e.g. non-action on Kashmir and Chechnya, has given way to 'active oppression' – the war on terror, and in Iraq and Afghanistan are all seen by a section of British Muslims as having been acts against Islam.

This disillusionment may contribute to a sense of helplessness with regard to the situation of Muslims in the world, with a lack of any tangible 'pressure valves', in order to vent frustrations, anger or dissent.[75]

The report, which was circulated among senior levels of the government, went on to add that for true radicals foreign policy served as a 'key driver behind recruitment by extremist organisations'.[76] In January 2005, a CIA report said that Iraq had become a training ground for international terrorists and that inevitably some of them would return to their country of origin.[77] Three months later, a document entitled 'International Terrorism: Impact of Iraq', that was agreed to by the heads of MI5, MI6 and Government Communication Headquarters (GCHQ), offered a dire description of the Iraq effect. 'It has reinforced the determination of terrorists who were already committed to attacking the West', said the report about the Iraq War, 'and motivated others who were not'. That danger would only continue: "Iraq is likely to be an important motivating factor for some time to come in the radicalisation of British Muslims and for those extremists who view attacks against the UK as legitimate.'[78]

The Iraq/foreign policy factor continued to be referred to by those in the know after the 7/7 bombings. On MI5's website in the days after the London atrocities appeared the following: 'Though they have a range of aspirations and "causes", Iraq is a dominant issue for a range of extremist groups and individuals in the UK and Europe.'[79] In a document created for Scotland Yard after the bombings, foreign policy was singled out as an important factor: 'Iraq HAS had a huge impact.' The report went on to point out that the relationship was more complicated than simply being one of cause and effect: 'Iraq is cited many times in interviews with detained extremists but it is over-simplistic to describe terrorism as the result of foreign policy. What western foreign policy does provide is justification for violence . . .' The ultimate solution to terrorism, according to the document, is a multi-faceted approach, including 'the removal of justifying causes (Palestine, Iraq), the erosion of perverted beliefs and day-to-day frustrations'.[80] Then there was the US National Intelligence Estimate from April 2006: 'The Iraq conflict has become the "cause célèbre" for jihadists, breeding a deep resentment of US involvement in the Muslim world and cultivating supporters for the global jihadist movement.'[81]

Despite what counter-terrorism experts had to say, the Blair government and media hawks believed that British foreign policy had not sparked an upsurge in terrorism.[82] 'Their cause is not founded on an injustice', declared the Prime Minister. 'It is founded on a belief, one whose fanaticism is such it can't be moderated. It can't be remedied. It has to be stood up to.' He added that the terrorists would exploit dissent over the war.[83] Charles Clarke labelled those making the link between terrorism and the Iraq invasion, including apparently British and American intelligence agencies, as being guilty of 'serious intellectual flabbiness'.[84] After all, went the refrain, the 9/11 attacks had occurred before the invasions of Afghanistan and Iraq. This, of course, did not represent a refutation of the argument that American and British foreign policy contributed to the sense of grievance that led some to participate in terrorism. There was a much longer history of western interference in the affairs of the region through coups (Iran), attempted coups (Syria), support for authoritarian regimes (Egypt, Saudi Arabia, Kuwait, Gulf States, Iraq), double standards when dealing with Israel (the treatment of Palestinians, the invasions of Lebanon in 1982 and 2006) and so on.[85]

Considerable evidence exists to the effect that the invasion of Iraq has actually made international terrorism worse. Consequently, the domestic British war against terror has become more difficult. There are the intelligence reports that Iraq is now a training ground for terrorists who will eventually take their new skills back to their home countries in an even more dangerous diaspora than the one spawned by Afghanistan.[86] Iraq since the invasion has become a source for generating revenues to aid al-Qaeda in building up its operations in its new base of Pakistan.[87] There is the reality that the invasion of Iraq, including the preparations leading up to it, had transferred important resources from the hunt for bin Laden and the war against al-Qaeda.[88] Finally, invading Iraq and the subsequent loss of hundreds of thousands of lives has played directly into efforts by bin Laden and al-Zawahiri to portray the American war on terror as part of the 'clash of civilizations' between Muslims and Christians.

Lastly, there is the statistical evidence. In a detailed study they called 'the Iraq effect', terrorism experts Peter Bergen and Paul Cruickshank found that 'the Iraq War has generated a stunning sevenfold increase in the yearly rate of fatal jihadist attacks, amounting to literally hundreds of additional terrorist attacks and thousands of civilian lives lost'. Even after excluding attacks that had occurred within Iraq and Afghanistan, they still found a 33 per cent increase in terrorism in the remainder of the world.[89] When it comes to terrorism, the ramifications of the invasion of Iraq and decades of western policies toward the region will be felt long into the future. Even Tony Blair acknowledged publicly in his official resignation speech that the Iraq War had led to 'blowback . . . from global terrorism and those elements that support it, [which] has been fierce and unrelenting and costly'.[90]

If there were divergent interpretations as to what motivated terrorists targeting the UK, needless to say a variety of opinions existed on the true significance of that menace. The numbers of terrorists in the UK fluctuated widely both before and after the 7 July bombings. The same individual who joined the government of Gordon Brown as an adviser on international security issues in June 2007 supplied several of the figures (see Table 3.1).

Table 3.1: Terrorism Figures as Quoted in the Media[91]

- 200 al-Qaeda supporters in the UK in 2001 (*The Times*, 2006)
- 'several hundred' terrorists (Tony Blair, *Women's Hour*, February 2005)
- 200 al-Qaeda terrorists in the UK (Lord John Stevens, 5 March 2005)
- 30 or 40 potential suicide bombers (security source, *Guardian*, March 2005)
- 'dozen or so' 'cleanskin' terrorists (Jason Burke, *Observer*, 13 March 2005)
- 3,000 British-born or British-based had been through al-Qaeda training camps (Lord Stevens, July 2005)
- 10,000 have gone to extremist conferences (*The Times*, July 2005)
- 16,000 based on 1% of British Muslims supporting 7 July bombings (July 2005)
- 300 British Muslims of Pakistani origin had joined al-Qaeda since 9/11 (*Kashmir Herald*, July 2005)
- 10,000 to 15,000 al-Qaeda supporters (*NY Times*, July 2005)
- 600 British men trained in al-Qaeda camps (*NY Times*, July 2005)
- 100,000 people from 'completely militarised' areas such as the Horn of Africa and Afghanistan who know 'how to use an AK-47' (*Independent*, August 2005)
- hundreds of terrorism suspects under MI5 surveillance (Charles Clarke to Parliament, September 2005)
- 700 al-Qaeda terrorists (MI5 source through *Independent*, May 2006)
- 8,000 al-Qaeda sympathizers (based on a figure of 0.5% of Britain's Muslim population being sympathetic to al-Qaeda) according to MI5 operation codenamed Project Rich Picture (*Independent*, July 2006)
- 'at least 700' al-Qaeda supporters (Whitehall source, *The Times*, July 2006)
- 300% increase in al-Qaeda supporters since 9/11 (*The Times*, July 2006)
- 200 terrorist networks involving 1,600 individuals (Dame Eliza Manningham-Buller, director general of MI5, November 2006)
- up to 120,000 British Muslims tacitly supporting terrorism (Sir Ian Blair, *Sunday Times*, November 2006)
- 100,000 'supporters of terror attacks' (*Financial Times*, December 2006)
- 3,000 individuals with al-Qaeda training camp experience in Britain (BBC, April 2007)
- 4,000 terrorists in the UK (Lord John Stevens, May 2007)
- 2,000 terrorists in the UK (MI5, according to Lord John Stevens, May 2007)
- 219 terrorist cells (MI5, *News of the World*, July 2007)
- '30 known plots . . . over 200 groupings or networks and around 2,000 individuals' (Gordon Brown, Parliament, July 2007)

The range of figures points to the difficulty in defining a terrorist. There is an enormous difference between: a) sympathizing with a terrorist cause; b) aiding a terrorist cause; and c) actually participating in a terrorist cause. The presence of sympathizers in the UK has led to the speculation that the number of terrorists could be in the thousands. Sympathizing does not automatically equal participation. Nor does involvement in terrorist training necessarily lead to carrying out violent acts. As a security source told the *Guardian*, 'Just because they have been to training camps does not mean to say they are going to be a suicide bomber.'[92]

Profiling terrorists is no easy task. The wide range of numbers being bandied around by the media, politicians and experts points to the need for any estimates to be treated with scepticism. A Dutch study of over 200 Muslims convicted or accused in connection to terrorism found nothing unique to distinguish them from the wider Muslim community.[93] Indeed, one of the major fears of policing and intelligence services is potentially how diverse the threat is. This diversity does not necessarily apply to overall numbers but terrorist groups have the potential of drawing on those who do not conform to terrorist stereotypes as a deliberate strategy for avoiding detection. This has occurred in a wide variety of places, ranging from Sri Lanka to Palestine to Chechnya, where terrorist groups have employed women as suicide bombers out of a belief that the scrutiny of them would be less intense.[94] In that sense creating a prototypical terrorist to be on an alert for is potentially self-defeating as terrorist groups respond in chess-like fashion to moves designed to stop them. Indeed, there is no better illustration of this than the failed terrorist attacks in London and Glasgow in June 2007. Those allegedly involved do not appear to conform at all to some of the dominant trends in previous British terrorism.

The diversity of the terrorism threat was reinforced in the 2006 American National Intelligence Estimate. The 'global jihadist movement is decentralized, lacks a coherent global strategy, and is becoming more diffuse', it warned. 'New jihadist networks and cells, with anti-American agendas, are increasingly likely to emerge. The confluence of shared purpose and dispersed actors will make it harder to find and undermine jihadist groups.' It added that the threat from 'self-radicalized cells will grow'.[95] The internet is an obvious force in allowing for the operation of such cells. This will only grow in the future, creating an increased likelihood of sustained but low-level terrorism not on the 9/11 scale.[96]

If there is any kind of pattern to some of the recent terrorism in the UK it is that Pakistan is a key factor. Some of this has to do with simple demographics – British Pakistanis, many of whom come from Kashmir, represent the second highest group of British Asians living in the UK (of the 1.6 million Muslims in Britain, 750,000 are Pakistani, mainly from Mirpur, part of Pakistani Kashmir).[97] This has led to strong ties between the UK and Pakistan, including frequent travel between the two places by an estimated 400,000 Britons a year.[98]

There are several reasons that might account for the involvement of some Britons of Pakistani heritage in terrorism. Pakistan's tensions with India over the Muslim-majority Indian Kashmir and the mistreatment of the Muslim minority in India (India has the second highest Muslim population in the world after Indonesia) plays into a sense of Muslims as the victims of repression at the hands of non-Muslims. Reportedly several hundred Britons fought in Kashmir during the 1990s as part of this cause and India's High Commissioner to the UK warned in 1994 of the involvement of young British Muslims in this type of activity.[99] Thus, Kashmir fits with other causes in the 1980s and 1990s such as Afghanistan, Palestine, Bosnia, Iraq in the era of sanctions and Chechnya that have radicalized and been used to radicalize young Muslims.[100] This argument conforms to Robert Pape's contention that suicide bombing is frequently connected to nationalism and oppression along ethnic and national lines rather than simply being about religion.[101]

There are, of course, other relevant factors. The treatment of Pakistani Muslims in the United Kingdom with respect to discrimination and racism, although by no means unique in relation to other groups, also contributes to a sense of alienation as does the confused place of second-generation British Pakistanis. These factors arguably make radicalism of any type more appealing – a majority of members of al-Muhajiroun between 2000 and 2003 were of Pakistani heritage. The radical organization once claimed to have funnelled a number of British Muslims into fighting for the liberation of Kashmir.[102]

Then there are the practical factors. Al-Qaeda, in whatever form it currently exists in, clearly now has at least parts of Pakistan as its primary base. It has worked on strengthening ties with Kashmiri terrorist groups of the type in which Britons have been active in the past, such as Lashkar-e-Taiba and Jaish-e-Muhammad.[103] Training camps have been established, thanks in part to revenue generated from illegal activities in Iraq, fostered by the breakdown of order associated with the UK/US invasion. Parts of Pakistan are virtual no-go areas for the Pakistani military allowing al-Qaeda or al-Qaeda-affiliated organizations the freedom to run the camps and for visits by individuals who would later be involved in terrorism back in the UK, including two of the 7 July bombers.[104] Pakistan's President Pervez Musharraf's decision to side with the United States and the United Kingdom in the immediate aftermath of 9/11 has fuelled opposition to him within Pakistan. So too have American and British actions, including the toppling of the Taliban, a government that Pakistan had strongly supported through its state intelligence agency. Largely because of its foreign policy, between 2002 and 2005, on average 17 per cent of Pakistanis had a favourable view of the United States.[105]

It is the Pakistan link to the UK, including what one official called a 'human pipeline' that sends some British Muslims there for terrorism training, that has concerned the American government as it considers new ways that al-Qaeda might strike at the USA. The fear is that the terrorist organization will use the UK as a conduit for such attacks. Problems on the part of British intelligence in monitoring the movement of Britons to Pakistan or in determining the full extent of the Pakistani links to the 7 July bombings and other terrorism plots, including alleged operations to bring down airliners using liquid gel explosives, have not reassured Washington.[106] Rumours in early 2007 suggest that Washington is considering requiring British Pakistanis to obtain special visas that are different from those of other British citizens in order to travel to the US. The Bush administration's Director of Homeland Security, Michael Chertoff, said publicly that his government feared the possibility of terrorist attacks carried out in the US by British or European so-called 'clean skins'.[107] The 2006 National Intelligence Estimate warned the Bush administration that terrorists saw 'Europe as an important venue for attacking Western interests' along the lines already carried out by 'extensive Muslim diasporas', such as Madrid and London.[108] The Brown government's July 2007 proposed creation of a border police force, a Conservative Party policy, is undoubtedly an effort to address this issue.[109]

It is also important to remember that other forms of terrorism remain and that it is possible to focus too heavily on Islam-related terrorism. In 2006 across the European Union there were over 500 terrorist incidents. A grand total of one, a suitcase bomb at a railway platform that failed to explode in Germany, had a link to Islam. Other forms of terrorism more directly connected to ethnic nationalism or separatism, which is what most of the attacks in Europe in 2006 consisted of, may grow in the future. Whatever the type of terrorism that exists, it is the security services and police forces that will be charged with battling them. Their tactics and the success of these will be the focus of the next chapters.[110]

On the day that London waited to find out whether it would host the 2012 Olympics, a meeting took place of great significance to the United Kingdom's counterterrorist efforts in the British war on terror. Dame Eliza Manningham-Buller, who had risen from her first job with the Security Service doing clerical work to be its director general, was providing a private briefing. In the course of her talk to 12 senior Labour Members of Parliament, she assured them that there was no imminent threat of attack to the United Kingdom in general or to London in particular. These types of meetings had occurred regularly since 9/11, although usually a less senior member of MI5 provided the briefing.[1] Hers was not the only word of reassurance. The next day, 7 July 2005, the most important police officer in the UK, Sir Ian Blair, the head of the Metropolitan Police, appeared on Radio 4's *Today* programme to discuss security requirements for the 2012 Olympics. 'We have been described by Her Majesty's Inspectorate of Constabulary as the envy of the policing world in relation to counter-terrorism', he proudly declared. When asked about the chances of an attack in London, Blair replied, 'It is difficult to calculate whether it is inevitable that they will get through.'[2]

In making these comments, the heads of two domestic security agencies reflected a wider institutional belief that the threat of terrorism had subsided by the summer of 2005. Two months earlier, the Joint Terrorism Analysis Centre (JTAC), the body charged by MI5 with analysing all intelligence available on terrorism and producing a threat assessment, had decided to reduce the then secret threat level to the United Kingdom from 'SEVERE GENERAL' to 'SUBSTANTIAL'.

The former meant an attack was a 'priority' and 'likely' while the latter only indicated it was 'likely'.[3] The decision was made on the basis of available intelligence that there was 'not a group with both the current intent and the capability to attack the UK'.[4] According to the parliamentary committee that investigated the matter, nothing available from either JTAC or the Joint Intelligence Committee (JIC), consisting of the heads of the three main intelligence agencies plus a variety of officials and senior civil servants drawn from around the government, contradicted the decision to reduce the alert level. There was the belief, 'it turned out wrongly', said Manningham-Buller, that high-profile arrests in 2004, in a case known as the 'fertilizer plot', had reduced the possibilities of a major coordinated terrorist strike within the UK.[5]

After 7/7, stories would initially emerge that those involved in the attacks had been completely unknown to British security agencies and police forces. These so-called 'clean skins' had emerged from obscurity in Leeds and Luton to carry out deadly suicide attacks that no one could possibly have anticipated. Eventually, of course, a more compli-cated picture began to emerge. At least two of the 7 July bombers, Mohammad Sidique Khan and Shehzad Tanweer, had been known to MI5. They had turned up in surveillance materials, including videos, recordings and pictures, as part of Operation Crevice, the investigation of Omar Khyam and his conspirators involved in the fertilizer bomb plot. At one point Khan had even been followed as he drove back to his parents after a meeting with Khyam. MI5 also possessed in its records the phone number of Jermaine Lindsay, although its signifi-cance would not emerge until after Lindsay had blown up himself and 26 others on the London Underground. The official explanation from the Intelligence and Security Committee for the failure to follow up these leads was that MI5, operating with limited resources, was required to make assessments based on risk factors.[6] Surveillance is expensive in terms of resources and human capital. Britain is not a police state, therefore by definition the number of individuals who can be spied on in terms of the commitment of resources and the awarding of special powers to the police and the Security Service is finite. In the case of Operation Crevice, for which Khan and Tanweer came to the attention of the Security Service and then were excluded, dozens of suspects had to be assessed.[7] Thus threat priorities needed to be established.

The handling of 7/7 did not offer a ringing endorsement of the capabilities of British counter-terrorism in the country's war on terror. Nevertheless, the government of Tony Blair rallied to the aid of MI5 and the police and deflected calls for the establishment of an independent public inquiry to investigate the bombings. The government response was fitting: in a democracy MI5 and the police function within a counter-terrorism environment created by politicians through legislation, budgets and policy decisions like the invasion of Iraq. Still, questions remain to be answered. What has the record of British counter-terrorism been since 9/11? How have the efforts been structured and funded? How soon did Britain respond to the growing threat of terrorism? What methods are the most effective at curtailing terrorism? What does the future of counter-terrorism hold?

The United Kingdom, of course, has dealt with terrorism since the nineteenth century. The UK's counter-terrorism experience with the current form of terrorism is more recent. It dates from the 1980s and principally from 1988 and the downing of Pan Am Flight 103 over Lockerbie, Scotland, which became an enormous policing and intelligence operation. Among those actively participating in the effort at Lockerbie was MI5 member Eliza Manningham-Buller.

The late 1980s and early 1990s were no ordinary period in the history of British intelligence. Its *raison d'être* for much of the twentieth century had been a death struggle with communism. For MI6, this meant working abroad against Soviet and Eastern Bloc interests. For MI5, it was work at home to counter Soviet and Soviet-allied intelligence efforts, both espionage and the more nebulous subversion. The centrality of these roles began to crumble by the early 1990s with the collapse of the Soviet Union and the emergence of Eastern Europe from communism. Although the threat did not completely disappear – Russia continues to operate a foreign intelligence service dedicated to espionage – the central focus of resources did. What would intelligence services do next? This was a question being asked in other western nations, including the United States, where the Central Intelligence Agency (CIA) began to pursue other roles, for instance fighting against the international drug trade.

For MI5, there was a similar scramble for a new focus. Because of the violence related to Ireland, it already as an intelligence organization had counter-terrorism experience. The MI5 Director General of the day, Stella Rimington, who took over in 1992, recognized that her organization needed to adjust its priorities in order to survive and prosper. She herself had served as director of counter-terrorism at MI5 at one point in her career.[8] As a result, she increasingly emphasized the importance of counter-terrorism, mainly connected to the IRA. In 1992, in a move criticized by some but which reflected recognition of how troublesome the activity had been for domestic intelligence agencies, MI5 disbanded its counter-subversion branch.[9] Resources were shifted from counter-subversion and counter-espionage into the Security Service's T Branch that focused on countering Ireland-related terrorism. It additionally had G Branch, a smaller body dedicated to countering international terrorism which would eventually grow to surpass T Branch. A change in mindset was required to move away from traditional perceptions of terrorism as being simply a criminal matter and thus the domain of the police. This view had been inherent in British counter-terrorism since the nineteenth century as witnessed by the lead role given to Special Branch over Northern Ireland.[10]

The growing threat in the 1990s of international terrorism combined with the endgame surrounding Northern Ireland increased the significance of agencies battling terrorism. With the end of the Cold War, MI5 suddenly emerged into the public spotlight in an unprecedented manner. In July 1993, Stella Rimington became the first head of the Security Service to be not just publicly named but to have her picture published. There was a new effort, generated in part by controversy surrounding MI5's activities as outlined in sources such as former member Peter Wright's *Spycatcher*,[11] to make the domestic intelligence agency more accountable. In 1994, John Major's government brought in the Intelligence Services Act. This legislation attempted to provide proper legal and political oversight of Britain's three main intelligence agencies: MI5; Government Communication Headquarters (GCHQ), charged with intercepting communications as part of a world-wide Anglo-American network; and MI6. The Act established rules around the use of warrants and also created the Intelligence and Security Committee composed of nine parliamentarians who would report directly to the prime minister on a yearly basis about the activities of the three main intelligence agencies.[12] It was in the same period that the Major government appointed Lord Lloyd of Berwick to review the Prevention of Terrorism Act. His recommendations would lead to the Terrorism Act 2000.

By 1994, the Security Service increasingly reflected its leader's desire for a greater emphasis on counter-terrorism. In that year, Rimington announced during a public lecture that nearly half of MI5's resources were now dedicated to counter-terrorism, with the primary focus being on Northern Ireland.[13] Of course, in dealing with counter-terrorism, MI5 was one of several important agencies. MI6 carried out operations against terrorists abroad, as did the military through the SAS. GCHQ intercepted communications connected to terrorism. Domestically, the Special Branch of the Metropolitan Police was the main police agency. The Metropolitan Police had by then established the Anti-Terrorist Branch that emerged out of its bomb squad.[14]

The real necessity, of course, with a multi-faceted system of counter-terrorism was coordination. A 1997 operation designed to stop an IRA bombing campaign in England required work by Special Branch, the Anti-Terrorist Branch and the Security Service to conduct thousands of hours of surveillance and compile nearly 5,000 pages of evidence.[15] In that sense counter-terrorism would remain the same in the 9/11 world except that the scale would change dramatically. Complex investigations involving multiple countries, a variety of types of communication, and numerous sources of intelligence, collectively equalled the need for a far more sophisticated form of British counter-terrorism and, arguably, greater resources.[16]

The system was not without its weaknesses. The obvious one was the danger in investing primacy in a single police force, namely the Metropolitan Police, allowing it to dominate and give a London-centric focus to British counter-terrorism. Thus, when terrorism acts occurred outside of the national capital the Metropolitan Police would, in the words of Deputy Assistant Commissioner Peter Clarke, 'gird up its loins and become an expeditionary force' since 'there was no unit, on the UK mainland, dedicated to the investigation of terrorism outside London'.[17]

By the 1990s, the threat posed by the IRA began to decline thanks to a political process but also the increasing effectiveness of British counter-terrorism, especially through the use of human intelligence.[18] Already international terrorism had emerged as a replacement. The Joint Intelligence Committee considered terrorism a 'First Order of Priority'. The 1998 bombings of the American embassies in Kenya and Tanzania provided ample evidence of the new threat posed by al-Qaeda. Tension heightened in December 1999 as the millennium neared. Arrests in Jordan and in the United States grabbed worldwide attention. By 2000, GCHQ had labelled Osama bin Laden as a 'major preoccupation' and, in June 2001, serious discussion about him and his organization took place as part of a joint US–UK intelligence summit. At the time the JIC produced an intelligence estimate warning that an al-Qaeda attack was in its final planning but that when or where it would occur was unknown.[19]

By the time of 9/11, Britain was in some respects well prepared because of its decades of counter-terrorism experience and the existence of new anti-terrorism legislation. The Terrorism Act 2000 offered additional powers to British counter-terrorism bodies beyond those provided in previous legislation. There was, for example, the authority to cordon off areas on the grounds of security. Under Section 41 of the Act, police gained a 'special arrest power for use in terrorist cases . . . where . . . there is not enough to charge an individual with a particular offence even though there is reasonable suspicion of involvement with terrorism'. The wide-ranging powers could and would be used against a number of targets. One who encountered this new law at first hand was Walter Wolfgang, a delegate to the 2005 Labour Party convention. He was briefly detained by police under the Terrorism Act after he shouted 'nonsense' during a speech by Foreign Secretary Jack Straw praising the Iraq invasion. Section 44 gave the police the authorization to stop vehicles and search the occupants in specified areas for specified periods of time.[20]

Then came 9/11. In the US, the attacks were a disaster for that nation's intelligence agencies. On the receiving end of budgets of tens of billions of dollars, the CIA and the Federal Bureau of Investigation (FBI) had failed to protect their country against attack. This failure largely occurred because of a problem with sharing and coordinating intelligence. Many of the pieces of the puzzle that would have allowed at least part of the 9/11 attacks to be foiled were available, but the CIA just would not share them with the FBI.[21] Spurred on by the 9/11 Commission, an open bipartisan public inquiry, radical reform would ensue, particularly for the FBI, which would shift its main priority from crime to terrorism, a point regularly referenced in the American television series *The Sopranos*. The Bush administration enacted several other fundamental changes. It created the Department of Homeland Security and gave it dominance over domestic security. A National Intelligence Directorate under the leadership of a National Intelligence Director was established in an effort to overcome structural problems that worked against the sharing of intelligence. Because of their collective failures, both the CIA and FBI lost power and prestige. The CIA suffered another blow over the perception that it had supplied flawed intelligence in the lead-up to the invasion of Iraq.[22]

For domestic intelligence services outside the United States, the impact of the terrorist attacks was neither as dramatic nor as negative. It could even be conceivably argued to have been positive. The now obvious peril posed by terrorism translated into governments offering to create new powers and provide additional resources to fight the menace. What did not radically change in the case of the UK, perhaps because there was no perceived need to change since Britain had not been hit by the terrorist attacks, was the structure of counterterrorism. In hindsight, the Blair government responded too slowly by falling back on new laws that revealed a reactive, short-term and politicized mentality.

This mentality prioritized fresh laws in the belief that holes existed in the Terrorism Act 2000. The clear emphasis in the new legislation was on foreign nationals with ties to terrorism living in the UK. The Anti-Terrorism, Crime and Security Act (ATCSA) allowed for the indefinite internment of foreign nationals who could not be deported. It also authorized the use of intercepted communications as evidence in appeals by groups against their proscription or individuals against their internment or deportation.[23] The use of deportation represented an effective form of counter-terrorism as recognized by MI5 itself since it allowed for the ejecting of a terrorism-related problem.[24] The same point applied to tightened immigration rules that would see over 200 foreign students barred from studying at British universities on security grounds between 2001 and 2005.[25] The early government emphasis created the impression that terrorism was primarily a foreign-related problem. The first arrests only reinforced this view. This also left British counter-terrorism on its back foot when it would eventually come to deal with a home-grown terrorism hazard.[26]

Another governmental response was to increase the resources going into British counter-terrorism, although a dramatic expansion would not occur initially. At the time of 9/11, the three lead intelligence agencies were all 2 to 3 per cent understaffed due to funding cuts in the 1990s. The Security Service soon sought to add an additional 130 members, mainly to be focused on intelligence collection, analysis and dissemination. Collectively, the three would see an emergency rise in their budgets by £54 million in 2001 to 2002 and a similar amount for the following fiscal year. These increases were not necessarily to be focused on counter-terrorism but, in fact, to ensure the maintenance of other core services because of the dramatic shift of resources into dealing with terrorism.[27] The government offered another major budgetary boost devoted to counter-terrorism in 2004. The Security Service was to receive 73 per cent of the increase, with the Secret Intelligence Service getting 21 per cent and GCHQ the remaining 6 per cent.[28]

By 2001–2, MI5, which employed around 2,000 people, dedicated 57 per cent of its budget to counter-terrorism with the majority of that

(32 per cent) still being devoted to terrorism related to Ireland. International terrorism accounted for 25 per cent of that figure while the next highest budgetary item was counter-espionage at 16 per cent. Only in the 2002 to 2003 period would the resources for countering international terrorism finally surpass that which went to Northern Ireland (see Table 4.1). Undoubtedly, there was a bureaucratic element to the slow shift in resources. Careers had been established and resources pumped into countering the IRA. Suddenly shifting to concentrate on a new target was no easy matter. There was a familiarity that came with battling Irish republicanism for more than a century. The same could not be said for international terrorism.[29]

Table 4.1: Partial Security Service Breakdown of Resources
Related to Counter-terrorism, 1997–2006

	Ireland-Related Counter-terrorism (%)	International Counter-terrorism (%)	Total Counter-terrorism (%)
1997–1998	19.5	16.4	35.9
1998–1999	–	–	–
1999–2000	–	–	50+
2000–2001	–	–	–
2001–2002	32	25	57
2002–2003	29	32	61
2003–2004	25	41	66
2004–2005	20	52	72

NB The numbers released by the Intelligence and Security Committee are incomplete.[30]

The Security Service had another crucial role to play when it came to counter-terrorism. That was in the area known to the UK government as 'Critical National Infrastructure'. Because of decades of actual (and potential) IRA attacks on parts of the British infrastructure, efforts had been made by the Security Service to identity over 400 vulnerable areas and work with people in these fields to improve security through training and providing expert advice including contingency plans designed by the Home Office.[31] This work has extended more broadly in society. MI5, for example, has advised major grocery chains on how to be on the lookout for shoppers making certain purchases, such as chemicals or mobile phones in bulk, to be used in bombs. They have also asked the same staff to watch for individuals who may be seeking to conduct a terrorist attack against a grocery store in order to cause major loss of life and widespread panic and economic damage. By 2007, the government was considering a plan to require state employees like properly vetted doctors and council workers to provide information to the authorities if they believed a violent crime is being planned. A similar program known as Operation TIPS was briefly floated by the Bush administration in 2002 before suggestions that it represented the creation of an East-German-style police state led to the program's elimination.[32]

When it came to intelligence agencies and domestic counter-terrorism, MI6 and GCHQ had significant but smaller roles to play than did the Security Service. In the initial post-9/11 period, MI6 nearly doubled its resources devoted to counter-terrorism, including transferring some of its personnel back to London. GCHQ also substantially raised its commitment to counter-terrorism. The agency doubled the number of personnel working against terrorism and shifted other resources to the point that for a period between 30 to 40 per cent of its total effort addressed the crisis.[33]

The significance of these intelligence agencies in the war against terrorism extended to their wider international relationships. In that relationship Britain depends on the United States for foreign intelligence for the simple reason that the US has a greater global reach with heavier resources to bring to bear.[34] Britain, through GCHQ, is, for instance, part of a global Anglo-American system that intercepts electronic communication. Other nation's intelligence services operating in regions of interest to the UK, like the Middle East, additionally aid British efforts against domestic terrorism, even in some cases supplying information obtained under torture.[35] One of the government's justifications for failing to investigate kickbacks surrounding an arms deal with Saudi Arabia was that it would not be in Britain's national interest because it might curtail the flow of needed intelligence about Islamic extremism.[36] Another important foreign relationship because of strong historic ties is that with Pakistan. This association's importance will continue for the foreseeable future because Pakistan has become the centre of the operations of the new al-Qaeda.[37]

Police forces are equally important to British counter-terrorism because of their presence on the ground and their ability to carry out arrests. Special Branch, of course, had been the original counter-terrorism police force. In the late 1970s, the Metropolitan Police added the Anti-Terrorist Branch as another tool for tackling terrorism. The drive toward a single counter-terrorism police force gained momentum only after 7/7. The Home Office amalgamated the Anti-Terrorist Branch (ATS or SO13) with the Metropolitan Police Special Branch (MPSB or SO12) to form a new single body for counter-terrorism called Counter Terrorism Command (also known as SO15). It came into existence as the UK's lead police counter-terrorism force on 2 October 2006.[38] A further 500 more members would be added to the new agency bringing its full strength to approximately 2,000. The actual division of duties within Counter Terrorism Command would largely continue as before. The remnant of Special Branch would perform intelligence-gathering while former members of Anti-Terrorist Branch would do the investigative work. In the event of a terrorist attack, as occurred at Glasgow International Airport on 30 June 2007, the local police will take the initial lead in consultation with Counter Terrorism Command. Since 7/7, three major regions, such as the West Midlands, have established their own Counter Terrorism Units.[39]

Then there was the senior administrative level that governed British counter-terrorism above and beyond the police and the Security Service. Thanks to Northern Ireland, a number of tried and established bodies were in place. These included the Cabinet Office Civil Contingencies Secretariat, the government's crisis planning committee known as COBRA, and the Joint Intelligence Committee. Some reform did occur after 9/11. In June 2003, the Joint Terrorism Analysis Centre was established. JTAC, which operates out of the Security Service headquarters, consists of representatives from 11 different government agencies and departments.[40] Additionally, the Blair government sought to improve counter-terrorism coordination by creating a new senior civil service position in the Cabinet Office in the form of Security and Intelligence Co-ordinator and Permanent Secretary. A veteran civil servant, Sir David Omand, who began his government career with GCHQ, got the initial job.[41] Finally, after the October 2002 Bali bombing, a new internal threat status alert system designed to provide more flexibility in determining the terrorism threat was created. Then in the aftermath of the 7 July bombings, the government adopted an American-style threat alert system by making the previously secret alert levels public.[42]

Then came the Home Office. Increasing troubles with it appeared over the course of the war on terror leading one Home Secretary to describe it as 'not fit for purpose'.[43] The Blair government decided to split it up as a result, with the idea being that the Home Secretary could focus more clearly on security, including countering terrorism, while other duties moved to a new Ministry of Justice. The government resisted Conservative demands for the creation of an American-style Homeland Security department. The Home Office did establish two new bodies for counter-terrorism as part of its reforms, however. One was an office for security and counter-terrorism within the Home Office, while the other was a body across several government policies and with its focus on Islamic extremism.[44]

When it comes to combating terrorism, new laws and administrative reforms are no substitute for boots on the ground. Actual resources to fight the war of terror at the micro level arrived surprisingly late. Not until February 2004 did the Home Office announce that the Security Service would see its staff numbers undergo a 50 per cent increase by March 2008 and that Special Branch would receive £3 million more a year to establish eight regional 'intelligence cells'. The latter expansion was an accurate recognition that London did not have a monopoly on terrorism.[45] The somewhat strange positioning of this growth, coming as it did in 2004, nearly two-and-a-half years after 9/11, did not generate controversy. However, the level of resources committed to British domestic counter-terrorism did finally become an issue after 7/7. The controversy revolved around the fact that additional surveillance of Mohammad Sidique Khan and Shehzad Tanweer had been dropped because MI5's limited resources required prioritization. Those connected to the fertilizer plot received the attention instead.[46]

The government retort to criticism of the delayed expansion of the Security Service was that recruiting people into an intelligence agency is no easy task. Indeed, stories appeared of efforts by al-Qaeda to infiltrate the ranks of the Security Service through the expansion.[47] Whatever the validity of this argument, it does not explain why the move to expand the Security Service did not occur until 2004. Nor does the response explain the slowness in initiating another important 2004 reform that would prove of even greater relevance within less than a year. In effect, admitting that counter-terrorism was too London-centric, the Security Service began an effort to establish regional offices around the country to work more closely with police forces. In connection to this shift, it set up a 'Northern Operating Centre' outside of London. After the actual attack on London on 7 July by terrorists based outside the city, this planned expansion grew from six to eight new regional offices designed to match the regional offices established by Special Branch.[48] The reactive quality to the measures remained, however.

The Blair government's broader counter-terrorism strategies also displayed a delayed response. Sparking the government into action were the March 2004 Madrid bombings. The attacks in the Spanish capital demonstrated in terrifying fashion that Europe, and thus Britain, had no special immunity from terrorism of the 9/11 variety. After Madrid, the Blair government introduced CONTEST, its main counter-terrorism strategy. CONTEST was a multifaceted five-year strategy designed to 'reduce the risk from International Terrorism so that our people can go about their business freely and with confidence'. Four areas were covered by the strategy: prevention, pursuit, protection and preparedness. 'Prevent' targeted the radicalization of individuals, including addressing inequality and discrimination and challenging radical ideologies that support terrorism. 'Pursue' pertained to improved intelligence, the disruption of terrorist activity and better coordination with Britain's international friends. 'Protect' meant improved domestic security of ports and public transportation systems. Finally, 'Prepare' addressed readying the UK to respond in the event of an attack.[49]

In applying these general principles, the Blair government recognized, even if the general public did not, that the complete elimination of terrorism was impossible. Containment, a Cold War notion that had once been directed at the Soviet Union and communism, was the path to be followed. This point was readily acknowledged by senior civil servant David Omand:

> We said that working together we will be able to reduce the risk from inter-national terrorism so that people can go about their normal business freely and with confidence . . . 'Reducing the risk': not eliminating it – no false promises to the public – so that people can go about their normal business – that's really the test because that's what the terrorists are trying to disrupt.[50]

Following through on at least one of the four principles was problematic. Part of 'Prevent' required addressing the 'root causes' of terrorism. To do so in practice was difficult for political reasons. Britain occupied a position dependent on the US when it came to foreign policy in the war on terror. UK interests had to conform to those of Washington even if, as in the case of the invasion of Iraq, they made Britain's domestic security in terms of terrorism worse. Nor was the pursuit of terrorists an uncomplicated assignment because resources, some of which still needed to be directed toward Ireland-related terrorism, were finite.[51] Members of the civil service were not enamoured with CONTEST. A leaked internal study in 2005 admitted that the Blair government's counter-terrorism strategy had largely been about discussion and symbolism and not concrete action: 'The strategy is immature. Forward planning is disjointed, or has yet to occur. Accountability for delivery is weak and real work impact is seldom measured.'[52]

As part of its approach to counter-terrorism, the British state also sought to ascertain the extent of the domestic problem posed by Islamic extremists and develop a program for reducing it. After the Madrid attacks, the Home Office and Foreign Office undertook a joint study into the extent and nature of Muslim extremism in the UK. The government received the report, entitled 'Young Muslims and Extremism', later the same year.[53] The Security Service and Special Branch began their own surveys of Islamic extremism in the aftermath of 7/7. MI5's work took place under the codename of Project Rich Picture. The effort was designed to monitor British Muslims prone to radicalization and thus potential recruits into terrorism. In style such ventures differed little from the Cold War when considerable resources went into monitoring those with the potential to be recruited by Communists. Despite not being launched until after the London bombings, it did deviate from the reactive quality of much of the government's approach to post-9/11 counter-terrorism. 'Rather than just firefighting', one official told the *Independent*, 'we are finding out the causes, why it's happening, why are people radicalised, and how they are radicalised, and then deal with some of these issues.'[54]

Another example of proactive counter-terrorism involved the then head of the Security Service, Eliza Manningham-Buller. In November 2006, to widespread media coverage, she publicly stated that MI5 was monitoring 1,600 people working within 200 terrorist networks and active in 30 plots, often under the control of al-Qaeda elements in Pakistan.[55] Speculation ensued as to why she had made her intervention. Did she wish to send a warning to the British public? Was she trying to generate greater resources for counter-terrorism? There was another possible motivation for her surprising comments that remained unmentioned. It connected counter-terrorism to counter-subversion in the Cold War. Then, from the perspective of the state, open Communists posed less of a threat since they could be monitored and contained. The real perceived danger came from the secret Communists, some of whom, like the 'Cambridge 5', had infiltrated the British government. The priority of intelligence agencies became to ascertain the identities of secret Communists or fellow travellers. Individuals associating with known Communists immediately fell under suspicion and were subjected to more intense surveillance to ascertain their leanings. Some would become confirmed Communists or Communist sympathizers. Others would remain suspected Communists and thus under continued mistrust. Some would be cleared.

The same principles applied to counter-terrorism investigations and were evident in the lead-up to 7/7. Mohammad Sidique Khan and Shehzad Tanweer became of interest to the Security Service after they had contact with some of the individuals involved in the fertilizer bomb plot. Khan and Tanweer were photographed and recorded. Khan was followed home. Police and the Security Service made inquiries about him. In the end, he was incorrectly deemed not to be a major threat and had the surveillance withdrawn. This decision came down to prioritizing because of limited resources. Surveillance, however conducted, is labour-intensive. Direct surveillance of a single individual can require as many as 60 people (up to three surveillance teams consisting of 15 to 20 personnel per team) over a 24-hour period.[56] This extrapolates to thousands of individuals to monitor the 1,600 individuals involved in the 30 plots that Eliza Manningham-Buller said were under surveillance in the autumn of 2006. Such coverage is beyond the scope of the Security Service and police, even with a larger workforce. As a result, the police have resorted to using military personnel to take part in surveillance operations, something previously seen in Northern Ireland. The interaction of the two bodies has led to tensions that may have contributed to the confusion which led to the mistaken killing of Jean Charles de Menezes.[57]

This brings the focus back to why Manningham-Buller made her surprising declaration. Her very comments represented a form of counter-terrorism. This is because it is the unknown, not the known operations currently under surveillance, that really concerns MI5. This is one of the reasons why the government has resisted banning the radical Hizb ut-Tahrir organization. It is easier to monitor the operations of any group and its known associates when they occur openly. With terrorism the concern pertains to the unknowns, the 'clean skins' operating in the shadows and readying to strike. By emphasizing that widespread surveillance is under way, Manningham-Buller was sending a message via the media to anyone remotely connected to terrorism or even radicalism: someone may be watching you. This was her point. MI5 cannot keep all potential terrorists under surveillance. By applying a figure to those involved in plots – and the figure was likely inflated since it is not in the interest of the Security Service to downplay the number – she had put those involved in radical activities on notice that the Security Service may be spying on them. Her words may have sparked paranoia and caution on the part of potential terrorists. Can I trust my colleagues working with me as part of the plot? Are we being followed? Are our conversations being listened to? The convicted ringleader of the fertilizer plot posed that very question to an underling: 'Do you think your room is monitored?' 'Do you know,' came the reassuring reply, 'I think we give them too much credit, bruv.'[58]

Manningham-Buller's public comments further reiterated that the domestic British war on terror is a massive undertaking. A year after the 7/7 attacks, police had compiled 13,353 witness statements and accumulated 29,500 exhibits and 6,000 hours of CCTV footage.[59] There was nearly a 20 per cent increase in the use of operations involving armed police officers between 2004–5 and 2005–6, mainly because of counter-terrorism operations. In 2006 alone, MI5 saw an 80 per cent increase in its case loads. In the same year, the Metropolitan Police had 70 terrorism investigations.[60] The work required the use of a variety of tactics. For example, in one 15-month period, from 2005 to 2006, police forces and intelligence services in the context of terrorism and other investigations made 439,000 applications for the monitoring of either telephones or electronic mail or the post. At least 4,000 of these were mistakes, including 67 involving the direct inter-ception of communication.[61] The authorities were not just listening in. Under the Terrorism Act 2000, police could carry out stop and searches. From 2002 to 2003, 21,500 of these occurred. From 2003 to

2004, the figure rose to nearly 30,000 and the following year it increased to almost 36,000.[62]

For British counter-terrorism agencies the results since 9/11 have been decidedly mixed. Ultimately, the practice represents a no-win situation. First, the broader context they have to function in is determined by politicians. Then there is the reality that for the police and MI5 any failures, such as actual terrorist attacks or botched arrests, are magnified exponentially. Terrorism expert Paul Wilkinson offers an apt British metaphor: 'Fighting terrorism is like being a goalkeeper. You can make a hundred brilliant saves but the only shot that people remember is the one that gets past you.'[63] On the other hand, many of their successes because of secrecy and the murky work of terrorism never earn a newspaper headline. Finally, failures do not roughly equate to successes; they are more detrimental in a number of key ways. A successful terrorist attack damages morale, weakens public and government confidence in counter-terrorism agencies, and can even lead to backlashes against minority populations that in the long run produce more terrorists. Botched raids or the inability to achieve convictions similarly damage morale, while alienating minority populations whose cooperation is crucial.

The counter-terrorism record of the Labour government is clearly a mixed one. There have been undeniable successes. Money destined for terrorism financing has been seized since the Anti-Terrorism, Crime and Security Act 2001.[64] Major terrorist operations have been disrupted. Operation Crevice, a massive and sophisticated undertaking, resulted in arrests and convictions over a serious bomb plot. The case of Dhiren Barot and individuals affiliated with him, involved in plotting bombings in the US and UK, also concluded with convictions. The government also effectively prosecuted those responsible for the failed bomb attacks of 21 July 2005. The ultimate success of the breaking up of an alleged plot to bring down a number of airliners through liquid explosives will be determined in a court of law, although the US media reported that British authorities were pressured by their American counterparts into launching the arrests before they were ready.[65]

Not all successes involve arrests. Frequent references to the disrupting of terrorism plots have appeared in the public domain. In December 2005, London Mayor Ken Livingstone said that ten terrorist plots had been stopped. These attacks consisted not of a 'great organised international conspiracy' but rather 'disorganised and small groups of disaffected people'. In early 2007, the *Sunday Telegraph* reported that security forces foiled a new plot roughly once every six weeks and that in total 12 plots had been discovered between July 2005 and January 2007.[66] Of course, plots varied in sophistication and the extent of the planning involved.

Then there were the failures. There was the ricin plot that did not fully pan out. The media loved the plan to bomb Old Trafford but it was anything but. The mistaken police killing of a Brazilian electrician harmed community relations while weakening confidence in the competence of those responsible for protecting the UK.[67] Equally damaging in these respects was a raid by over 250 police officers on two homes in Forest Gate in London that ended with the arrests of two brothers and the shooting of one of them. Media stories, fuelled by leaks from the police, suggested that a chemical attack was being planned.[68] Instead, the police had accidentally shot an innocent man who along with his brother was released without charge. The police subsequently issued an apology, although they defended the raid and the Independent Police Complaints Commission supported them. However, the damage to British counter-terrorism was undeniable.[69] Finally, came the arrests in Birmingham for an alleged plot to kidnap a British Muslim soldier, behead him and post the video on the internet. Of the nine men arrested to much media fanfare as part of Operation Gamble, three were later released without charge, and only one was accused of the alleged kidnapping.[70]

Statistically, there was a clear pattern to terrorism arrests. First, the majority of those arrested were eventually released without being charged.[71] Even then, those being charged faced only a small probability that they would ever be convicted. Between 11 September 2001 and 31 March 2007, the police detained 1,228 people on suspicion of involvement in terrorism (see Table 4.2). From these arrests 241 people were eventually charged under some form of terrorism legislation and 41, or less than 4 per cent of the total arrests, were eventually convicted. However, some of the charges have yet to come to trial, while others found themselves accused of a different crime. The first person accused for the failed attack on Glasgow Airport in June 2007 was charged under the Explosive Substances Act 1883, a piece of legislation introduced because of Fenian bomb attacks.[72]

Table 4.2: Percentage Outcome of Arrests under Terrorism Act 2000, 11 September 2001 to 31 March 2007[73]

Result	No.	%
Charged with terrorism offences only	132	10.7
Charged with terrorism legislation offences and other criminal offences	109	8.9
Charged under other legislation including murder, grievous bodily harm, firearms, explosives offences, fraud, false documents	195	15.9
Handed over to immigration authorities	76	6.2
On police bail awaiting charging decisions	15	1.2
Warrant issued for arrest	1	0.08
Cautioned	12	1.0
Dealt with under youth offending procedures	1	0.08
Dealt with under mental health legislation	11	1.0
Transferred to Police Service of Northern Ireland custody	4	0.3
Remanded in custody awaiting extradition proceedings	2	0.16
Awaiting further investigation	1	0.08
Released without charge	669	54.5
Total	1228*	100**

*This figure includes 1165 arrested under the Terrorism Act 2000 and 63 that occurred under other legislation as part of a terrorism investigation
**Percentages do not add up exactly to 100% due to rounding.

Topping everything was the ultimate counter-terrorism failure: the 7 July bombings. The fact that two bombers, who had been under state surveillance that stopped when they were deemed not to be a serious threat, killed 56 people including the bombers, and injured hundreds did not generate faith in the competence of British counter-terrorism. Nor did the headlines that appeared over subsequent months: 'Spies "Hid" Bomber Tapes from MPs'; 'Revealed: MI5 Ruled London Bombers Were Not a Threat'; 'U.S. Says Informant Flagged London Bomber'; 'New Clues Support Al-Qaeda Theory for London Bombing'; 'Ministers "Shocked" at MI5's Lack of Information'; 'Terror Alert Downgraded, Then Attacks Came Out of the Blue'; 'June Report Led Britain to Lower Its Terror Alert'; 'MI5 Told MPs on Eve of 7/7: No Imminent Terror Threat'.[74] Collectively the disaster that was 7/7 should have led to an independent inquiry, not only to reassure the families of the victims but to restore confidence that British security was fit for purpose. Although valuable, the review by the Intelligence and Security Committee lacked the broad canvas and transparency of the American 9/11 Commission. As a result, some questions about 7 July will never be properly answered and doubt will always remain, particularly as to whether the attacks could have been prevented. Adding to the need for a public inquiry are the failed London transportation attacks of 21 July 2005 and the apparent failed car attacks in London and Glasgow at the end of June 2007. As with 7/7, British counter-terrorism appears to have been taken by surprise.[75]

While 7/7 demonstrated the danger of terrorism to the UK, the refusal of the government to hold a proper independent inquiry is damaging to British counter-terrorism. Successful counter-terrorism in a democratic society requires trust and confidence in the efficacy of security forces because public cooperation is essential. Much of that assistance is earned through capturing so-called 'hearts and minds', particularly in some of the communities where terrorists are to be found, confronted and contained.

A brief media and political firestorm erupted in the United Kingdom in April 2007. Its spark was the words of veteran police officer Deputy Assistant Commissioner Peter Clarke, the head of Counter Terrorism Command. In a highly publicized speech, he criticized leaks to the media made prior to counter-terrorism arrests that occurred in Birmingham in January 2007. Inherent in Clarke's criticism, some believed, was that the leaks had occurred for political reasons and represented further evidence of the politicization of terrorism. Ignored in the same speech, however, was a far more important point for British counter-terrorism. Clarke admitted that Britain was losing the war for 'hearts and minds'. This was not an explicit admission on his part. Rather it was made implicitly when he lamented the inability of British counter-terrorism to generate domestic human intelligence:

> We must increase the flow of intelligence coming from communities. Almost all of our prosecutions have their origins in intelligence that came from overseas, the intelligence agencies or from technical means. Few have yet originated from what is sometimes called 'community intelligence'. This is something we are working hard to change.[1]

Clarke's remarks were echoed in July 2007 by the former head of the Security Service Dame Eliza Manningham-Buller, who called for the recruitment of networks of, in the words of *The Times*, 'Muslim spies'. Her intervention strongly indicates that her former organization had failed to do this already.[2] Her comments followed immediately on the heels of similar remarks by the new minister for counter-terrorism in the government of Gordon Brown, Admiral Sir Alan West. He went so far to advocate 'snitching or talking about someone . . . because the people we are talking about are trying to destroy our entire way of life'.[3]

The ultimate significance of their collective remarks was a simple one: Britain is failing to generate domestic human intelligence because it is losing the war to capture 'hearts and minds'. This despite the fact that it is crucial for the UK's future safety to win over communities from which terrorists spring, find recruits or receive nourishment. The reasons for this are manifold, including structural weaknesses on the part of those charged with the UK's security. Ultimately, however, the responsibility lies at the feet of the elected politicians who have too often since 9/11 allowed the domestic war on terror to be driven by short-term political considerations instead of long-term strategic needs that address the 'root causes' of grievances felt by some in Muslim communities and which the government itself is well aware of.[4]

There is no question as to the significance of 'hearts and minds' when it comes to containing terrorism, argues scholar Thomas R. Mockaitis:

Historical evidence and contemporary experience suggest that terrorism is a weapon and not an end in itself. The current struggle should, therefore, be seen as a counterinsurgency campaign against an organization with very specific regional objectives based upon a larger ideological goal. Such an organization can only be defeated with precise intelligence that allows for the highly focused and limited use of force. This intelligence can only come from the larger communities in which the insurgent terrorists operate. Members of these communities must be encouraged rather than coerced to cooperate in the struggle. They will be motivated to do so only if they see such action as substantially and materially bettering their lives. Addressing the urgent needs and legitimate grievances of such a population can provide such motivation. There is no substitute for an effective hearts-and-minds campaign.[5]

The campaign for 'hearts and minds' generates intelligence and that, according to Paul Wilkinson, is the 'secret of winning the battle against terrorism in an open democratic society'.[6] Wilkinson's point has been echoed at the highest levels of British counter-terrorism. Sir David Omand, who would retire as Security and Intelligence Co-ordinator in April 2005, told a Radio 4 programme what his advice to the Prime Minister about counter-terrorism strategy would be:

> I would say, 'Remember, Prime Minister, that pre-emptive secret intelligence is the key to success. So you are going to have to enable your intelligence services to acquire that information and, at the same time, we've got to encourage the community to volunteer information, as they reject the extremists and their ideology. So you have to accept the necessity of some intrusive surveillance and investigation – which means you have to do so under proper oversight – and maintain community confidence in the actions of the state, including in the protection that they have from the framework of human rights and the quality of justice.'[7]

Human intelligence emerges from a number of sources. It could be obtained through the infiltrating of an organization from the outside in the form of an agent, as in the case of an intelligence officer going undercover. This is easier said than done. In the case of the current war on terror, the police and/or intelligence services would largely be infiltrating Islamic groups, predominantly Asian or British Asian in makeup. There were structural obstacles that blocked this from occurring either overseas or at home. One principal problem was the fact that the agencies doing the infiltrating lacked diversity. MI5, for example, remains far from reflecting modern Britain. Only 6 per cent of its members were drawn from ethnic minorities at the end of 2006, although it did manage to recruit 14 per cent of its 400-person intake for the same year from ethnic minorities. The Metropolitan Police Service, in charge of one of the most ethnically diverse cities in the world, was not much better with just under 8 per cent of its officers drawn from ethnic minorities.[8]

An equally noteworthy source of human intelligence comes from the targeted communities themselves in what Peter Clarke calls 'community intelligence'. This could be in the form of volunteered intelligence, such as ringing the local police station with a tip-off regarding suspicious activity. It might even involve an individual volunteering or being recruited by the authorities while already part of a terrorist cell or being injected into a cell from the outside. These informers offered the potential for supplying extremely detailed and important raw intelligence on the inter-workings of terrorist cells and radical groups. Several alleged terrorism plots broken up in Canada and the United States since 9/11 prominently featured intelligence supplied by informers, either through initial tip-offs or by being employed by the police and intelligence agencies within the groups being investigated.[9]

By Clarke, Manningham-Buller and West's own admissions, Britain has not generated a desired level of human intelligence. Why has British counter-terrorism failed to obtain human intelligence and/or why have communities not supplied it? The fact that members of the intelligence and police services do not reflect the communities they are seeking information from is one obvious factor. Even more important has been the seeming inability to win over the communities where some of the terrorists emerge from and where the intelligence to foil terrorism needs to come from as well.

At one time the motivations needed to generate human intelligence were more straightforward – money was a key one. This was true in the wider Cold War from the 1950s on as widespread idealism about communism vanished with Nikita Khrushchev's denunciation of Josef Stalin.[10] That was then, however: this is now. The threat of communism has been replaced by terrorism. Terrorists often do not resemble the vast majority of police and intelligence officers, in terms of ethnicity, language, religion and culture.[11] Kinship and familial ties also make terrorist cells more impenetrable to infiltration. Finally, there is the reality of dealing with terrorists who often have a religious motivation, which in the extreme makes them prepared to die for their cause. Recruiting informers requires finding a motivation, but what possible motivation could be offered to an individual who looks forward to the afterlife even if getting there requires blowing himself and others up? The task is a difficult one. The more likely approach is to infiltrate someone from the outside into the targeted organization assuming an outsider could play a believable terrorist to the point where his or her comrades would reveal information. Cumulatively, all of these factors help explain why it is difficult to generate human intelligence about the current terrorism threat within the UK.

Failure to generate human intelligence, moreover, spoke to a broader truth beyond the lack of capabilities or limitations on the part of an intelligence service when it came to generating such material. Most types of human intelligence requires cooperation. And cooperation requires accommodation in the form of members of communities believing that it is in their interests to assist the authorities against other members of their community. That human intelligence has not been forthcoming in this way indicates a more systematic failure in the British war on terror.

Some will argue that the failure to garner more community support is little to do with the British government and everything to do with the communities in question. And yet opinion polling shows that the vast majority of those in British Muslim communities want nothing to do with violence and terrorism and are loyal to the UK.[12] Six surveys between November 2001 and March 2004, for example, found that between 7 and 15 per cent believed the 11 September attacks were justified versus 67 to 85 per cent who did not.[13] A year after the 7 July bombings, one survey found only 7 per cent of British Muslims who viewed the four bombers as martyrs while 16 per cent thought the action wrong but the cause correct.[14] A Gallup survey involving face-to-face interviews with British Muslims in the Greater London region relayed that 81 per cent opposed the use of violence even if the cause was just and were more trusting of government and the police than other communities.[15] Other surveys have revealed strong differences in social attitudes between British Muslims and non-Muslims with the former being far more conservative and thus at odds with majority opinion, although not necessarily with some on the British right.[16] Questions also remain about the willingness to integrate into the so-called mainstream, although one detailed survey of students at three schools in East Lancashire found British Muslims far more tolerant and open-minded than comparable white students and a joint Home and Foreign Office report admitted that a 'strong Muslim identity and strict adherence to traditional Muslim teachings are not in themselves problematic or incompatible with Britishness'.[17] The emphasis on integration as a significant factor in reducing terrorism may also be misguided. A Manchester University examination of the background of 75 Muslims charged in the UK with terrorism offences found that they were less likely to come from predominantly Muslim areas as opposed to more ethnically mixed areas. This reiterates again the difficulty in developing a clear and consistent portrait of post-9/11 terrorists.[18]

Reiterating the significance of the political context to counterterrorism, factors related to government policy have also contributed to the difficulty in winning 'hearts and minds'. British foreign policy since 9/11 has unquestionably damaged community relations in the UK. The invasion of Iraq is an obvious factor and opinion polls support this, but the way the American war on terror has been fought (extraordinary rendition and the use of torture under another name) has contributed to the worldwide decay.[19] Particularly destructive in this respect have been the images of the American prison camp at Guantanamo Bay and the seeming unwillingness of the Blair government to challenge Washington publicly over it until at least 2006, even though British citizens were being held there. Instead, members of MI5 were sent there to question them.[20] In the end, when the British citizens, most noticeably Moazzam Begg, came home they were released without charge, leaving the lasting impression that they are innocent men who lost months or years of their lives to American injustice and British government indifference.

The tone of the Blair government at various points had also worked against winning 'hearts and minds' through clumsy and/or ill-considered efforts that moved toward demonizing some or all British Muslims. A then minister in the Foreign Office, Dennis MacShane, called upon British Muslims in 2003 to choose between the 'British way' and 'terrorism'. He quickly disavowed his comments after myriad complaints.[21] Hazel Blears, while a junior minister in the Home Office, took the rhetoric to a new level in 2005. She insensitively told a parliamentary committee that British Muslims would simply have to accept that 'some of our counter-terrorism powers will be disproportionately experienced by' them.[22] Her words proved accurate. Stop and search had disproportionately targeted members of visible minorities. Nor was the evidence strong that the measures, with their echoes of tactics used in Northern Ireland, were useful. In the first nine months of 2006, 22,700 stops led to 27 terrorism-related arrests. The Metropolitan Police Authority described the program as doing 'untold damage' to community relations and also to perceptions of the police. Metropolitan Police chief Sir Ian Blair has promised a review of the use of this power.[23]

Another questionable step in winning hearts and minds occurred in 2006. A senior government minister, Jack Straw, suddenly made the wearing of the niqab a major topic of discussion among politicians and the media. The debate was quickly cast as being part of the failure of Muslims to integrate and failure to integrate was seen by some as one of the factors that had led to the involvement of British Muslims in terrorism.[24] In choosing to politicize the wearing of the niqab, little thought seemed to have been given by the government as to how this would aid in gaining more support from Muslim communities. Only 13 per cent of Muslims in London, according to one poll, believed that integration required the removal of the niqab.[25]

More germane to the need to win support of Muslim communities than criticizing women over niqabs was that the same poll found that 28 per cent of Muslims in London had experienced racial or religious discrimination in the previous year. A 2004 Islamic Human Rights Commission survey found that 80 per cent of respondents had encountered some form of discrimination. An internal government document drawn up before 7 July listed discrimination and economic destitution as factors in Muslim alienation.[26] Muslims themselves believed that Islamophobia was present in the British media, which regularly portrayed their religion in a negative light. Among those recognizing the legitimacy of these feelings of discrimination have been an assistant commissioner with the Metropolitan Police and the leader of the Conservative Party, David Cameron. The latter argued that 'racism and soft bigotry' needs to be tackled because '[y]ou can't even start to talk about a truly integrated society while people are suffering racist insults and abuse, as many still are in our country on a daily basis'.[27]

Even more damaging to community relations are the heavy-handed tactics enacted or proposed by the government and occasionally carried out by the police.[28] The system of control orders has seen

individuals put under de facto house arrest without facing charge or trial.[29] Statistically the majority of those arrested under the Terrorism Act 2000 since its inception have been released. A small percentage will be charged under the Act and only a much smaller number, under 4 per cent, will ever be convicted of a terrorism offence.[30] That equates to the lives of hundreds of innocent people being disrupted by the police. Botched raids such as Forest Gate and the police killing of Jean Charles de Menezes have damaged relations between the police and ethnic minority communities. Abu Bakr, a British Muslim arrested in Birmingham in January 2007 as part of an alleged kidnap plot, was just as quickly released without charge, leading him to label his country as a 'police state'. Other prominent British Muslims have criticized the government's approach to counter-terrorism as being counterproductive.[31] It is in this context that proposals to bring in powers to allow the police to stop and question anyone on the street, a tactic previously used in Northern Ireland, or a 90-day detention period without charge for individuals arrested under the Terrorism Act need to be judged.[32] Former intelligence officer Crispin Black explains the important criteria for assessing the utility of such legislation:

> Everything we do in response to terrorism should have two factors in mind. One is hearts and minds and the other is the flow of intelligence . . . If you [sic] sitting, say, in a Muslim part of Yorkshire and you are looking at your telephone thinking those three young men that I saw last night outside

the garage, maybe I should phone the police? And you've suddenly been presented with the fact that they can be detained for 90 days, does that make you more or less likely to produce that information to the authorities?[33]

His point was reinforced by a retired senior policeman and counter-terrorism expert: 'every time the [state] takes . . . extreme action against terrorism it drives more angry young men and women into the terrorist network.'[34]

The Blair government did try to engage with British Muslims but these efforts were inconsistent and largely emanated from the bureaucracy and not, likely for political reasons, from senior politicians. A joint Home Office/Foreign Office study entitled 'Young Muslims and Extremism' was launched in the aftermath of the Madrid bombings. It found that a variety of factors, including British foreign policy, were responsible for the radicalization of British Muslims. The Foreign Office's Islamic issues adviser, Mockbul Ali, even recommended granting a visa to radical Qatari cleric Sheikh Yusuf al-Qaradawi for a visit to the UK because of his opposition to terrorism in the West, even though he supported the use of terrorism against Israel and in opposition to the occupation of Iraq and had bigoted views towards gays and lesbians. Some within the government and police opposed the banning of the radical Islamic group, Hizb Ut-Tahrir, proposed by Blair in August 2005. 'I see no reason why HT should be banned on the basis of available evidence', said a representative of the Association of Chief Police Officers (ACPO). 'I haven't seen anything suggesting they have apologised for or glorified terrorism. I might not like their views but that doesn't mean that they are criminal and that is an important distinction we have to make.'[35]

One of the major obstacles in the way of a concerted effort to win hearts and minds is the post-9/11 dominance of the 'clash of civilizations' interpretation of terrorism. Surveys between 2001 and 2004 discovered that 57 to 70 per cent of British Muslims believed that the American and British war on terror was a war against Islam.[36] Efforts have been made to break free of this view; the Brown government's decision after the failed London and Glasgow attacks of June 2007 to avoid using the labels Muslim and Islamic in the context of the terrorism are part of this effort. This approach, however, is not as novel as the media suggests. Then Home Secretary John Reid, in a September 2006 speech, went out of his way to move away from depicting the conflict as Islam versus the West:

> The fight against terrorism is . . . a conflict of values, not a conflict of religions, not a clash of civilisation, it is not Islam versus the rest or the rest versus Islam. It is a conflict of values with the terrorists on one side and most modern civilisation is on the other side. It is a conflict between modern Islamic and values archaic [sic] and intolerant values. It is a conflict within Islam, as well as a conflict outside it. It is a fight against extremism, intolerance and terror, and not one against Islamic values and teaching.[37]

This was also the point to a speech by Hilary Benn in which he discouraged the use of the phrase 'war on terror' while attempting to encourage some understanding of the 'root causes' of post-9/11 terrorism.[38] Any form of measured response, however, quickly opens the government to allegations that it is engaging in appeasement. Leading the charge in this respect has been Melanie Phillips. She is largely a marginalized figure within her own country, but is influential in right-wing circles in the United States where her views affect conservative perceptions of the UK.[39]

In the aftermath of 7/7, the Blair government promised a new spirit of consultation with Muslim communities about how to tackle extremism in the UK. A series of working groups were set up and went to work in late August. A first sign that their findings would not have much of an impact on government policy occurred on 26 July 2005 when Blair denied a key motivation – and one recognized by his own government – that fuelled radicalization, especially of young Muslims:

> There is no justification for it period and we will start to beat this when we stand up and confront the ideology of this evil. Not just the methods but the ideas. When we actually have people going into the communities here in

this country and elsewhere and saying I am sorry, we are not having any of this nonsense about it is to do with what the British are doing in Iraq or Afghanistan, or support for Israel, or support for America, or any of the rest of it. It is nonsense, and we have got to confront it as that. And when we confront it as that, then we will start to beat it.[40]

Then, the following week, without waiting for the groups to even start, Blair announced his own 12-point plan to go after terrorism in the UK.[41] In that sense his approach was prescient as the final report issued by the government-appointed panels ran counter to the message that has been consistently put out by the government in the aftermath of 7/7. Their final conclusions downplayed the significance of mosques as a cause of radicalization while providing alternative explanations for the root causes of extremism:

> The Working Groups are united in the view that whilst the remit for various working groups was to tackle extremism and radicalisation, most if not all the strands see that the solutions lie in the medium to longer term issues of tackling inequality, discrimination, deprivation and inconsistent Government policy, and in particular foreign policy. Emphasis has also been placed repeatedly on the need to look not only at the events that occurred on those two days in July, but to the causes behind them. The Working Groups are therefore united in calling for a Public Inquiry in order for all the issues to be considered and examined in the public domain. The inquiry will be instrumental in understanding and learning from what has happened in order to prevent its reoccurrence.[42]

The experience seems to have convinced the government that it was pointless to work with Muslim organizations like the Muslim Council of Britain. Instead, then Communities Secretary Ruth Kelly set out to meet directly with community leaders and made it clear that public funding would only go to those groups that pursued the approved path.[43] Along those lines, the government floated proposals that would have targeted Islamic extremists at universities, in part by enlisting lecturers and other staff to spy on them, encouraged parents to spy on their children, and proposed setting up a 'joint information unit', modelled after a similar body used in Northern Ireland, to counter al-Qaeda propaganda.[44]

These approaches, of course, ignored the deeper issues in favour of short-term solutions. Until the government seeks to engage in an essential way with the 'root causes' of Muslim alienation, including foreign policy, the battle for 'hearts and minds' will remain a failing proposition. A report by the think tank Demos, the research partially funded publicly, argued that the government has been afraid to address fundamental issues because to do so would give the appearance that there might be some legitimacy to the terrorist cause or that the government might be complicit in what had occurred. Instead, reflecting a system caught between bureaucrats trying to address root causes and politicians fearful of an adverse media reaction, the government, argued the report, conveyed confusion that did nothing to make Britain safer from terrorism:

> In the meeting rooms of Whitehall, ministers were assuring Muslim leaders of the need for partnership, but in press briefings they were talking of the need for Muslims to 'get serious' about terrorism, spy on their children and put up with inconveniences in the greater good of national security.[45]

Terrorism has had a long past in the United Kingdom and, undoubtedly, will enjoy a lengthy future. As long as grievance of any sort exists, be it connected to nationalism or religion or any other cause, some individuals will turn to violence. It should go without saying, but in these times of ideological fervour it cannot, that there is no justification for terrorism ever. To create exceptions is to begin the slippery slope toward rationalizing violence. To understand the 'root causes' of terrorism is not, however, to justify it. Instead, it is an effort to understand this form of violence, and, hopefully, reduce such occurrences of it in the future.

The question then becomes: what is the appropriate state response to the violence? There are short-term and long-term approaches to take. The short term will invariably be dominated by laws, crackdowns and an emphasis on the role to be played by police forces and intelligence services. The long term requires greater government participation. If it decides, as in the case of Northern Ireland, that some legitimacy to the underlying grievances exists then negotiations may be the path to follow. If the demands are deemed unacceptable then a different course will need to be pursued ad infinitum.

Whatever the case, new acts of terrorism in the UK are a matter of when, not if. Already since 7 July, two potentially major terrorist attacks have been averted because of apparent technical failures on the part of the bombs or the detonators. Such luck will not continue indefinitely, whereas terrorism as a tactic will, since at its most basic it is a tool to be used by the weak against the powerful. Realistic discussions, then, about counter-terrorism will centre on the containment of

terrorism and not its elimination. In the future the goal of governments will be to ensure that when terrorism does occur it is on the
scale of a 7/7 and not a 9/11.

It is the contention of this book that the response of the former
government of Tony Blair to the current terrorism menace was inade-
quate, inconsistent and too often driven by the concerns of politics
instead of the needs of security. This point stretches all the way back
to the months after 9/11 when the government, and more specifically
it seems Tony Blair himself, made the decision to cast its lot with the
foreign policy pursuits of the Bush administration over Iraq. In doing
so, the issue of the United Kingdom's security became of secondary
concern to maintaining a strong relationship with Washington. In
pursuit of this agenda the threat posed by Iraq to the UK was exaggerated to sell the toppling of Saddam Hussein. Now, the phantom
monster of Iraq-fuelled terrorism has become a real one with bloody
fangs. The ramifications of this foreign policy disaster will be felt for
years to come in what one intelligence official nicknamed a 'bleed-
out' when the foreign and Iraqi terrorists operating in that decimated
country leave to look for new targets. Already, according to American
intelligence, al-Qaeda may be looking to use Iraq as a springboard for
attacks against the USA. There is also an apparent Iraq link to the
recent failed June 2007 terrorist attacks in the UK.[1]

The overselling of the threat of Saddam Hussein's Iraq represents a
microcosm of the Blair government's approach to the domestic war on
terror. At times, the Prime Minister and his government seemed to
prefer the appearance of dealing with terrorism as opposed to actually
doing anything about it. Hence the reactive resort to repeated pieces
of legislation and grandstanding, portraying measures like a 90-day
detention period without charge for those arrested under the
Terrorism Act and identity cards as tools for preventing terrorism. Why
the government took such an approach is reflected in opinion polls
and politics. At the time a large majority of the British public favoured
both identity cards (80 per cent) and 90-day detentions (72 per cent);[2]
the opposition parties did not. The government also found support
from the UK's highest-selling and most influential newspaper, *The*

Sun. The tabloid launched its own personal campaign in support of what amounts to a three-month internment without charge; it even used the image of a wounded 7/7 victim on its front page, who it turned out was opposed to that part of the legislation, in support of its chest-thumping and ironically entitled slogan 'Tell Tony He's Right'.[3]

The pattern for the use of 7/7 was established at Tony Blair's 5 August 2005 press conference. After an initial measured and co-operative response to the atrocities, he chose a different path. Blind-siding the opposition and even his own Home Secretary, he launched a get tough campaign that was praised by *The Sun* but in the long run lacked substance and has largely run aground. One of his promises that day was to ban the radical Muslim organization Hizb ut-Tahrir. At Gordon Brown's initial Prime Minister's Questions, one of David Cameron's first questions was why this had not occurred. It was left to former Home Secretary John Reid to point out later that the govern-ment lacked the required evidence to do so.[4]

Debates around identity cards or 90-day detentions distract from discussing measures and issues that might have made a difference with regard to 7/7 and future 7/7s. Why did the start of a substantial expansion in the number of members of MI5 and in its UK regional capabilities not occur immediately after 9/11 instead of in early 2004? Had the commitment of resources, a small fraction of what went into invading Iraq, occurred earlier it is not beyond the realm of possibility to suggest that MI5 could have kept two of the 7 July bombers under surveillance instead of having to wash their hands of them. On the other hand, perhaps the problem lay with the criteria employed by the Security Service in making such risk assessments. Instead of 90-day detentions, debate should be rampant over why the Security Service was unaware of the attacks of 21 July 2005 and late June 2007 that apparently failed only due to good luck. An independent and open public inquiry to investigate these matters is clearly needed. It would make the United Kingdom safer in both the short and long term by answering some of these crucial questions in the exact way that the 9/11 Commission in the United States did.

It is on the future that the focus must now be. The key to dealing with what will come is straightforward enough. It must be recognized that with the current terrorism there is a small core of radicalized individuals bent on carrying out acts of violence. What government policy must ensure is that these individuals are kept marginalized within their communities. They must not be allowed to lead others along the path of violence. If they are isolated then they can be contained, either by the state or by their own communities. Without a support network, they pose a much smaller threat. This is the lesson of Northern Ireland. The IRA was relatively marginalized in the 1960s but rose to be seen by many in the Catholic community as its defenders because of internment, Bloody Sunday, biased policing, anti-Catholic discrimination and other heavy-handed tactics. The result was an escalation of the violence, a decades-long conflict, and more than 3,000 deaths.

Prime Minister Gordon Brown is well aware of what needs to be done. This is true despite his continued support for identity cards and yet more anti-terrorism legislation, now with 56-day instead of 90-day detentions. There is also his inability to acknowledge that the decision to invade Iraq, not just the handling of the occupation, was a mistake. Brown understands that the key to anything approaching a long-term solution is, to quote him from an appearance on Radio 4's *The World at One*, and at the Hay Literary Festival, 'winning hearts and minds' and 'separating the extremists from the moderates'.[5] The difficulty is how to do this. It is much easier to lose 'hearts and minds' by alienating people through ill-thought-out and rushed policies driven by political interests and loyalties: launching an unnecessary invasion of Iraq and maintaining troops as part of what has become a bloody civil war; unquestioning support for the failed foreign policy of a failed American presidential administration; a lack of an even-handed approach to the Middle Eastern conflict, as witnessed by the inability of the Blair government to properly criticize Israel over its excessive response to a Hezbollah attack on a group of Israeli soldiers; supporting corrupt governments in the region; heavy-handed police tactics that destroy community relations; support of draconian domestic policies like detention for 90 days without charge; attacks on for what some amount to core religious and cultural practices. At best, alienation leads to a lack of crucial cooperation in the pursuit of human intelligence; at worst it can push the undecided into the terrorist camp.

There will always be extremists, some of whom cannot be reasoned with and must face the full powers of the state. But they are a tiny minority. What they must not be allowed to do is grow in numbers through recruitment. One of their tools for recruiting is to portray Muslims as being discriminated against and targeted by western countries including the UK. The invasion of Iraq, whatever the rightness of the cause and even the benefits for ordinary Iraqis, was counterproductive in terms of the war on terror because it played into the hands of extremists. It provided them with evidence for their claim that a 'clash of civilizations', a core belief of Osama bin Laden, was under way. The attack on minority cultural practices fits the same category. It is a recruiting sergeant for extremists in the same way that internment, anti-Catholic discrimination and Bloody Sunday provided the IRA with oxygen.

The key to long-term containment of terrorism, beyond practical policing and security measures designed to detect and defeat plots, is to reduce the supply of terrorists. Accordingly then, before introducing any new war on terror policy the British government should ask one fundamental question: does the measure contribute to winning 'hearts and minds'? If the answer is no, then the policy should be scrapped. The new Brown government appears to be open to such an approach. In its handling of the failed attacks in London and Glasgow in June 2007, it has demonstrated at least initially a more considered strategy than its predecessor. It did so by pursuing a low-key response that scrupulously avoiding invoking Islam in connection to the attacks so as not to demonize British Muslims. And it sought to portray the terrorists as criminals to deny them greater power and credibility than they deserve.[6] Whether such a measured and thoughtful approach can be maintained in the face of a sustained and vitriolic right-wing media assault and in the aftermath of future successful terrorist attacks remains to be seen.

Notes

Introduction

1 Home Office website, www.homeoffice.gov.uk/security/current-threat-level/, accessed 30 April 2007.

2 'UK terror threat now "critical"', BBC News, 30 June 2007, http://news.bbc.co.uk/1/hi/uk/6257606.stm, accessed 1 July 2007.

3 http://www.whitehouse.gov/news/releases/2001/09/print/20010920-8.html, accessed 1 May 2007.

4 Hilary Benn, 'Where Does Development Fit in Foreign Policy?' Department for International Development, 16 April 2007, www.dfid.gov.uk/news/files/Speeches/foreign-policy-april07.asp, accessed 25 April 2007.

5 Lord Carlile, 'The Definition of Terrorism' (London: Home Office, 2007) www.homeoffice.gov.uk/documents/carlile-terrorism-definition?view= Binary, accessed 25 March 2007.

6 David C. Martin and John Walcott, *Best Laid Plans: The Inside Story of America's War against Terrorism* (New York: Harper & Row, 1988), 53; Bruce Hoffman, *Inside Terrorism* (New York: Columbia University Press, 2006), 16.

7 Noam Chomsky, 'Terror and Just Response', Znet, 2 July 2002, www.zmag.org/content/showarticle.cfm?ItemID=2064, accessed 30 April 2007.

8 Samuel P. Huntington, *The Clash of Civilizations and the Remaking of World Order* (New York: Free Press, 1996), 210.

9 www.commondreams.org/headlines04/0109-02.htm, accessed 5 February 2007.

10 John Mueller, *Overblown: How Politicians and the Terrorism Industry Inflate National Security Threats, and Why We Believe Them* (New York: Free Press, 2006); Peter Oborne, *The Use and Abuse of Terror: The Construction of a False Narrative on the Domestic Terror Threat* (London: Centre for Policy Studies, 2006); Simon Jenkins, 'They See It Here, They See It There, They See Al-Qaeda Everywhere', *Sunday Times*, 29 April 2007.

11 Mueller, *Overblown*, 2–3.

12 Peter L. Bergen, *The Osama Bin Laden I Know: An Oral History of Al Qaeda's Leader* (New York: Free Press, 2006), 392.

13 Gilles Kepel, *The War for Muslim Minds: Islam and the West* (Cambridge, MA: Belknap Press, 2004), 123.

14 Peter Bergen and Paul Cruickshank, 'The Iraq Effect: War Has Increased Terrorism Sevenfold Worldwide', *Mother Jones*, 1 March 2007.

15 The four are: '(1) Entrenched grievances, such as corruption, injustice, and fear of Western domination, leading to anger, humiliation, and a sense of powerlessness; (2) the Iraq "jihad;" (3) the slow pace of real and sustained economic, social, and political reforms in many Muslim majority nations; and (4) pervasive anti-US sentiment among most Muslims.' 'Declassified Key Judgments of the National Intelligence Estimate, Trends in Global Terrorism: Implications for the United States', April 2006. www.globalsecurity.org/intell/library/reports/2006/nie_global-terror-trends_apr2006.htm, accessed 18 March 2007.

16 'Leaked Report Rejects Iraqi al-Qaeda Link', BBC News, 5 February 2003, http://news.bbc.co.uk/1/hi/uk/2727471.stm, accessed 10 March 2007; 'C.I.A. Aides Feel Pressure in Preparing Iraqi Reports', *New York Times*, 23 March 2003.

17 For examples of the equating of terrorism with cultural differences, see Melanie Phillips, *Londonistan: How Britain Is Creating a Terror State Within* (London: Gibson Square, 2006), 274–82, or Melanie Phillips, 'When Will the British Stop Appeasing Terror?' *Daily Mail*, 1 May 2007.

18 President George W. Bush, 'Address to a Joint Session of Congress and the American People', 20 September 2001, www.whitehouse.gov/news/releases/2001/09/20010920-8.html, accessed 20 June 2005.

19 James Fallows, 'Bush's Lost Year', *Atlantic Monthly*, October 2004.

20 Michael Scheuer, as quoted by Fallows (ibid.).

21 'Declassified Key Judgments'.

Chapter 1

1 'Telegrams: Attempted Rescue of Fenian Prisoners in London', *New York Times*, 14 December 1867.

2 Peter Berresford Ellis, *A History of the Irish Working Class* (London: Pluto Press, 1985), 140; Bernard Porter, *Plots and Paranoia: A History of Political Espionage in Britain, 1790–1988* (London and New York: Routledge, 1992), 96–7.

3 Porter, *Plots and Paranoia*, 101–2.

4 Peter Clarke, 'Learning from Experience – Counter Terrorism in the UK since 9/11', Colin Cramphorn Memorial Lecture, 24 April 2007.

5 Melanie Phillips, 'The Soft Brainlessness of Denying "Islamist Terror"', www.melaniephillips.com/diary/?p=1514, accessed 16 May 2007; David Cameron, 'What I Learnt from My Stay with a Muslim Family', *Observer*, 13 May 2007; Melanie Phillips, 'Britain's War Against...Well, You Know', *USA Today*, 10 July 2007.

6 Jason Bennetto, Colin Brown, Nigel Morris and Kim Sengupta, 'Security Services Identify 700 Potential Al-Qa'ida Terrorists at Large in Britain', *Independent*, 10 May 2006; Stephen Fidler, 'Britain under Threat from

Resurgent Al-Qaeda Security Forces Warn That 1,600 Operatives Are Plotting Attacks Here and Abroad', *Financial Times*, 7 December 2006; Matt Weaver, 'US "Wants British Pakistanis to Have Entry Visas"', *Guardian*, 2 May 2007.

7 Robert Pape, *Dying to Win: The Strategic Logic of Suicide Terrorism* (New York: Random House Trade Paperbacks, 2005), 3–24.

8 Peter Chalk and William Rosenau, *Confronting the "Enemy within": Security Intelligence, the Police, and Counterterrorism in Four Democracies* (Washington DC: Rand Corporation, 2004), 7.

9 Porter, *Plots and Paranoia*, 101–2; Bernard Porter, *The Origins of the Vigilant State: The London Metropolitan Police Special Branch before the First World War* (London: Weidenfeld & Nicolson, 1987), 27–8.

10 Porter, *The Origins of the Vigilant State*, 19.

11 'Timeline: Ireland', BBC News, 29 June 2007, http://news.bbc.co.uk/1/hi/world/europe/country_profiles/1038669.stm, accessed 2 July 2007.

12 'Sinn Feiners Raid Houses in London', *New York Times*, 16 May 1921.

13 Peter Hart, *The I.R.A. at War, 1916–1923* (Oxford and New York: Oxford University Press, 2003), 142–65.

14 Hart, *The I.R.A. at War*, 177.

15 The legislation, as quoted in Hart, *The I.R.A. at War*, 172; Michael Hassett, 'Irish Nationalists, the British Government and Anti-Terrorist Legislation', paper presented at the European Social Science History Conference, Amsterdam, March 2006, 2–3, 5.

16 Hart, *The I.R.A. at War*, 174–5; Hassett, 'Irish Nationalists', 2–3, 5, 10; J. Bowyer Bell, *The Secret Army: The IRA, 1916–1979* (Dublin: The Academy Press, 1979), 147–51.

17 Richard English, *Armed Struggle* (London: Macmillan, 2003), 60–1; Hassett, 'Irish Nationalists', 11; Bell, *The Secret Army*, 147–50.

18 Bell, *The Secret Army*, 156–60.

19 Hassett, 'Irish Nationalists', 12.

20 Bell, *The Secret Army*, 160–1.

21 Tony Geraghty, *The Irish War: The Military History of a Domestic Conflict* (London: HarperCollins, 1998), 3–4.

22 Thomas R. Mockaitis, *British Counterinsurgency in the Post-Imperial Era* (Manchester and New York: Manchester University Press, 1995), 97; Conflict Archive on the Internet (CAIN), http://cain.ulst.ac.uk/hmso/scarman.htm, accessed 18 February 2007.

23 For more on the riots, see 'Violence and Civil Disturbances in Northern Ireland in 1969 – Report of Tribunal of Inquiry', April 1972, CAIN, http://cain.ulst.ac.uk/hmso/scarman.htm, accessed 18 February 2007.

24 Porter, *Plots and Paranoia*, 198–9.

25 Frank Kitson, *Low Intensity Operations: Subversion, Insurgency, Peace-Keeping* (London: Faber and Faber, 1971), 49–50.

26 Peter Taylor, *Brits: The War against the IRA* (London: Bloomsbury, 2002), 53–5, 127.

27 Geraghty, *The Irish War*, 7, 29; Richard English, *Armed Struggle* (London:

Macmillan, 2003), 136; Bell, *The Secret Army*, 383; Tim Pat Coogan, *The IRA* (London: HarperCollins, 2000), 345; Taylor, *Brits*, 50.

28 Taylor, *Brits*, 57.

29 Taylor, *Brits*, 67; English, *Armed Struggle*, 139–40; Tim Pat Coogan, *The Troubles: Ireland's Ordeal, 1966–1996 and the Search for Peace* (London: Hutchinson, 1995), 126.

30 Taylor, *Brits*, 65; Mockaitis, *British Counterinsurgency in the Post-Imperial Era*, 122.

31 Willie Whitelaw, as quoted in English, *Armed Struggle*, 141.

32 'Internment – Summary of Main Events', CAIN, http://cain.ulst.ac.uk/events/intern/sum.htm, accessed 8 May 2007; Mockaitis, *British Counterinsurgency in the Post-Imperial Era*, 102, 108; Bell, *The Secret Army*, 382; Coogan, *The IRA*, 342; English, *Armed Struggle*, 123.

33 Taylor, *Brits*, 107.

34 Coogan, *The IRA*, 342–5; Bell, *The Secret Army*, 383; English, *Armed Struggle*, 151; Taylor, *Brits*, 107; Paul Wilkinson, *Terrorism Versus Democracy: The Liberal State Response* (Abingdon, Oxford and New York: Routledge, 2006), 82–3; Geraghty, *The Irish War*, 29.

35 Mockaitis, *British Counterinsurgency in the Post-Imperial Era*, 108.

36 Bell, *The Secret Army*, 405–6; Coogan, *The IRA*, 385–6; Mark Hollingsworth and Nick Fielding, *Defending the Realm: MI5 and the Shayler Affair* (London: André Deutsch, 1999), 134.

37 Steve Hewitt, *Spying 101: The RCMP's Secret Activities at Canadian Universities, 1917–1997* (Toronto: University of Toronto Press, 2002), 9–10.

38 Coogan, *The IRA*, 385–6.

39 Statewatch, 'UK Terrorism Act 2000: New Definition of "Terrorism" Can Criminalise Dissent and Extra-Parliamentary Action', September–October 2000, www.statewatch.org/news/2001/sep/15ukterr.htm, accessed 15 May 2007.

40 Hassett, 'Irish Nationalists', 12.

41 'List of Proscribed Terrorist Groups', Home Office, www.homeoffice.gov.uk/security/terrorism-and-the-law/terrorism-act/proscribed-groups, accessed 15 February 2007.

42 Roy Jenkins, as quoted in Taylor, *Brits*, 175.

43 Tony Blair as quoted in Tom Baldwin, 'From Liberal Lawyer to the Leader Taking Civil Liberties', *The Times*, 7 March 2005.

44 Bell, *The Secret Army*, 408.

45 Coogan, *The IRA*, 390–1; English, *Armed Struggle*, 170.

46 'The Year London Blew Up', www.channel4.com/history/microsites/H/history/t-z/year.html, accessed 14 April 2007.

47 Mockaitis, *British Counterinsurgency in the Post-Imperial Era*, 112.

48 Hollingsworth and Fielding, *Defending the Realm*, 122.

49 Porter, *Plots and Paranoia*, 199.

50 Hollingsworth and Fielding, *Defending the Realm*, 123.

51 Wilkinson, *Terrorism Versus Democracy*, 74; Hollingsworth and Fielding, *Defending the Realm*, 122.

52 Geraghty, *The Irish War*; Mark Urban, *Big Boys' Rules: The Bestselling Story of the SAS and the Secret Struggle against the IRA* (London: Faber and Faber, 1992, 105; David Millward, 'Mobiles Crucial to Tracking Suspects', *Daily Telegraph*, 4 July 2007.

53 British military commander as quoted in Urban, *Big Boys' Rules*, 101.

54 Mockaitis, *British Counterinsurgency in the Post-Imperial Era*, 108.

55 Taylor, *Brits*, 150.

56 Urban, *Big Boys' Rules*, 102, 244; Steven Greer, *Supergrasses: A Study in Anti-Terrorist Law Enforcement in Northern Ireland* (Oxford: Clarendon Press, 1995), 41–2; Louise Richardson, *What Terrorists Want: Understanding the Terrorist Threat* (London: John Murray, 2006), 54; Angelique Chrisafis, 'Mystery of Sinn Féin Man Who Spied for British', *Guardian*, 17 December 2005; Martin Ingram and Greg Harkin, *Stakeknife: Britain's Secret Agents in Ireland* (Dublin: The O'Brien Press, 2004), 16, 39, 83–93, 120–1; Coogan, *The IRA*, 519; Urban, *Big Boys' Rules*, 103–4; Annie Machon, *Spies, Lies and Whistleblowers: MI5, MI6 and the Shayler Affair* (Sussex: The Book Guild, 2005), 1.

57 Liam Clarke, 'New MI5 Chief Named in Probe over Murder of Policewoman', *Sunday Times*, 18 March 2007; Ingram and Harkin, *Stakeknife*, 39–40.

58 Taylor, *Brits*, 150–1.

59 Urban, *Big Boys' Rules*, 104–5; Ingram and Harkin, *Stakeknife*, 37.

60 Liam Clarke, 'Focus: The Spy at the Heart of the IRA', *Sunday Times*, 18 December 2005.

61 Mockaitis, *British Counterinsurgency in the Post-Imperial Era*, 121; Coogan, *The IRA*, 519.

62 Sandra Laville, 'Investigation Could Reveal Hand Behind Four Ulster Murders', *Guardian*, 10 April 2007; Statewatch, 'What Did "Bob" Do with FRU?', Britain's Force Research Unit, March 2007, www.statewatch.org/news/2007/mar/05northern-ireland-fru-MI5.htm, accessed 14 May 2007.

63 Urban, *Big Boys' Rules*, 106; Ingram and Harkin, *Stakeknife*, 15; Enda Leahy, 'MI5 "Helped IRA Buy Bomb Parts in US"', *Sunday Times*, 19 March 2006.

64 Allan A. Jackson, *Ireland, 1798–1998: Politics and War* (Oxford: Blackwell, 1999), 404; Taylor, *Brits*, 271; Geraghty, *The Irish War*, 158.

65 English, *Armed Struggle*, 207.

66 Coogan, *The IRA*, 516.

67 'Provisional IRA's History of Violence', BBC News, 1 September 1998, http://news.bbc.co.uk/1/hi/events/northern_ireland/paramilitaries/162714.stm, accessed 12 February 2007.

68 Conor Cruise O'Brien, 'Thinking About Terrorism', *Atlantic Monthly*, June 1986.

69 Matthew Teague, 'Double Blind', *Atlantic Monthly*, April 2006.

70 Hollingsworth and Fielding, *Defending the Realm*, 138–9.

71 Clive Walker, 'The Bombs in Omagh and Their Aftermath: The Criminal Justice (Terrorism and Conspiracy) Act 1998', *The Modern Law Review*, 62

(6) (November 1999): 879–902.

72 Michael Gove, *Celsius 7/7: How the West's Policy of Appeasement Has Provoked Yet More Fundamentalist Terror – and What Has to Be Done Now* (London: Weidenfeld & Nicolson, 2006), 45, 47.

73 'Statistics on the Operation of Prevention of Terrorism Legislation for 2000', Home Office, 13 August 2001, www.homeoffice.gov.uk/rds/pdfs/hosb1601.pdf, accessed 14 February 2007.

74 Liam Clarke, 'Sting by Security Services Foils Renewed Real IRA Campaign', *Sunday Times*, 25 June 2006; Michael Evans, 'Top Secret Intelligence Unit Will Quit Belfast for New Role in Iraq', *The Times*, 18 April 2005.

Chapter 2

1 'Tony Blair's Press Conference', 5 August 2005, www.number10.gov.uk/output/Page8041.asp, accessed 10 January 2007.

2 '9/11 Panel: Al Qaeda Planned to Hijack 10 Planes', CNN, 17 June 2004, http://edition.cnn.com/2004/ALLPOLITICS/06/16/911.commission/, accessed 14 November 2006.

3 Brian Jenkins, 'International Terrorism: A New Mode of Conflict', in David Carlton and Carlo Schaerf (eds), *International Terrorism and World Security* (London: Croom Helm, 1975), 16; Brian Jenkins, 'Nuclear Terrorism and Its Consequences', *Society* (July–August 1980), 6–8; Brian Jenkins, as quoted in Robert Pape, *Dying to Win: The Strategic Logic of Suicide Terrorism* (New York: Random House Trade Paperbacks, 2005), 345.

4 Tony Blair, as quoted in Michael White and Patrick Wintour, 'Blair Calls for World Fight against Terror', *Guardian*, 12 September 2001.

5 Ibid.

6 'World Marks September 11', BBC News, 11 September 2002, http://news.bbc.co.uk/1/hi/world/americas/2250513.stm#image, accessed 14 May 2007.

7 President Bush's 'Address to a Joint Session of Congress and the American People', 20 September 2001, www.whitehouse.gov/news/releases/2001/09/20010920-8.html, accessed 14 December 2006.

8 'Tony Blair's Speech', *Guardian*, 2 October 2001.

9 Statewatch, 'UK Terrorism Act 2000: New Definition of "Terrorism" Can Criminalise Dissent and Extra-Parliamentary Action', *Statewatch Bulletin*, 10 (5) (September–October 2000).

10 Clare Dyer and Alan Travis, 'UK Challenges Strasbourg Ban', *Guardian*, 12 July 2007.

11 Richard Norton-Taylor, 'Asylum Seeker Wins Damages', *Guardian*, 17 November 2004; Richard Norton-Taylor, 'Blair Intervened in Deportation Process', *Guardian*, 16 November 2004; Statewatch, 'UK: Egyptian National "Unlawfully Detained" after Intervention by Prime Minister', August–October 2004, www.statewatch.org/news/2004/nov/blair.pdf, accessed 11 January 2007.

12 Paul Wilkinson, *Terrorism Versus Democracy: The Liberal State Response* (Abingdon, Oxford and New York: Routledge, 2006), 80.

13 George Monbiot, 'A Glut of Barristers at Westminster Has Led to a Crackdown on Dissent', *Guardian*, 6 March 2007.

14 'Terrorism Act 2000', 20 July 2000, www.opsi.gov.uk/acts/acts2000/20000011.htm, accessed 27 March 2007.

15 Statewatch, 'UK Terrorism Act 2000'; Richard Norton-Taylor, 'Guilty until Proven Innocent', *Guardian*, 19 February 2001.

16 Jack Straw, as quoted in Hugo Young, 'Democracy is in Crisis if We Have to Rely on the Lords', *Guardian*, 18 December 2001.

17 Jack Straw, as quoted in Statewatch, 'UK Terrorism Act 2000: 21 New Proscribed Organisations', October 2001, www.statewatch.org/terrorlists/terrorlists.html, accessed 11 April 2007.

18 Sarath Wijesinghe, 'Laying It All on the Table', *Sunday Observer* (Sri Lanka), 3 June 2007, www.sundayobserver.lk/2007/06/03/fea01.asp, accessed 4 June 2007; Statewatch, 'UK Terrorism Act 2000: 21 New Proscribed Organisations'.

19 'Antiterrorism Law Protects Tyrants and Dictators', *The Times*, 20 February 2007.

20 Richard Norton-Taylor, '21 Groups Banned under New Terror Law', *Guardian*, 1 March 2001; Statewatch, 'UK Terrorism Act 2000: 21 New Proscribed Organisations', 2001; Home Office List of Proscribed Organizations, October 2001, www.statewatch.org/terrorlists/terrorlists.html, accessed 11 April 2007; www.homeoffice.gov.uk/security/terrorism-and-the-law/terrorism-act/proscribed-groups, accessed 14 May 2007.

21 Statewatch, 'UK Terrorism Act 2000: 21 New Proscribed Organisations', 2001; Home Office List of Proscribed Organizations, October 2001.

22 'Home Secretary to Ban Terror Groups', Home Office, 17 July 2006, http://press.homeoffice.gov.uk/press-releases/ban-terror-groups, accessed 12 March 2007; Home Office List of Proscribed Organizations, May 2007, www.homeoffice.gov.uk/security/terrorism-and-the-law/terrorism-act/proscribed-groups?view=Standard, accessed 30 May 2007; www.homeoffice.gov.uk/security/terrorism-and-the-law/terrorism-act/proscribed-groups, accessed 14 May 2007.

23 http://frwebgate.access.gpo.gov/cgi-bin/getdoc.cgi?dbname=107_cong_public_laws&docid=f:publ056.107.pdf; www2.parl.gc.ca/HousePublications/Publication.aspx?pub=bill&doc=C-36&parl=37&ses=1&language=E&File=19, accessed 12 January 2007; www.justice.gc.ca/en/news/nr/2001/doc_28217.html, accessed 12 January 2007; 'Australian Terrorism Law', www.aph.gov.au/library/intguide/law/terrorism.htm#2002, accessed 1 May 2007.

24 'Anti-Terrorism, Crime and Security Act 2001', 14 December 2001, www.opsi.gov.uk/acts/en2001/2001en24.htm, accessed 23 January 2007.

25 Ibid.

26 Ibid.; David Blunkett, as quoted in Patrick Wintour, 'Blunkett under Fire from All Sides on Terror Bill', *Guardian*, 20 November 2001.

27 Colin Nicholls, 'The UK Anti-Terrorism Crime and Security Act 2001: Too Much . . . Too Soon', Commonwealth Human Rights Initiative, February 2002, www.humanrightsinitiative.org/publications/nl/articles/uk/uk_anti_terrorism_crime_security_act_2001.pdf, accessed 12 May 2007.

28 'UK Pilot Was Arrested Despite FBI Call for 9/11 Secrecy', *Guardian*, 26 September 2005; Karen McVeigh, 'Pilot Held Over 9/11 Fails in Compensation Fight', *Guardian*, 23 February 2007.

29 Tania Branigan, 'Cleared Chef Says He Was Terror Case Scapegoat', *Guardian*, 10 August 2002.

30 'Checks on Terrorism Laws', Home Office, www.homeoffice.gov.uk/security/terrorism-and-the-law/checks-on-laws2/?version=8, accessed 14 July 2007.

31 Peter Clarke, 'Learning from Experience – Counter Terrorism in the UK since 9/11', Colin Cramphorn Memorial Lecture, 24 April 2007.

32 Simon Jenkins, 'A Sledgehammer for a Nut', *The Times*, 15 April 2005; BBC News, 'The Ricin Case Timeline', 13 April 2005, http://news.bbc.co.uk/1/hi/uk/4433459.stm, accessed 16 April 2007; Duncan Campbell, 'The Ricin Ring That Never Was', *Guardian*, 14 April 2005.

33 Tony Blair, as quoted in Richard Norton-Taylor, 'London and Washington Used Plot to Strengthen Iraq War Push', *Guardian*, 14 April 2005.

34 'U.S. Secretary of State Colin Powell Addresses the U.N. Security Council', www.whitehouse.gov/news/releases/2003/02/20030205-1.html, accessed 23 November 2006; 'Powell Calls Pre-Iraq U.N. Speech a "Blot" on his Record', *USA Today*, 8 September 2005; Richard Norton-Taylor, 'London and Washington Used Plot to Strengthen Iraq War Push', *Guardian*, 14 April 2005.

35 'Guantanamo Prisoner "Admits UK Terror Plots"', *Independent*, 15 March 2007.

36 Philip Cardy and Andy Russell, 'Man U Suicide Bomb Plot', *The Sun*, 20 April 2005.

37 Tariq Panja and Martin Bright, 'Man U Bomb Plot Probe Ends in Farce', *Observer*, 2 May 2004.

38 Peter Clarke, 'Learning from Experience'.

39 Peter Oborne, *The Use and Abuse of Terror: The Construction of a False Narrative on the Domestic Terror Threat Plus Indy Article* (London: Centre for Policy Studies, 2006), 25. The text of Hayman's letter is at http://p10.hostingprod.com/@spyblog.org.uk/blog/2005/11/asst_met_commissioner_andy_hay.html, accessed 10 June 2007.

40 For example, see 'Al-Qaeda Terrorists "on UK Streets"', *Daily Telegraph*, 6 March 2005. Also see the next chapter for examples of the widely varying numbers of terrorists in the UK.

41 Simon Jenkins, 'I Never Thought I'd Say This, but Thank You to the Lords, the Libs and the Law', *The Times*, 22 December 2004; Matthew Taylor, 'ID Cards Useless, Says Ex-Spy Chief', *Guardian*, 17 November 2005; Andrew Phillips, 'ID Cards Will Provoke a National Identity Crisis', *Observer*, 12 February 2006.

42 Lord Rooker, as quoted in Statewatch, 'UK Arrests and Detentions under Terrorism Laws', May 2002, www.statewatch.org/news/2002/may/11ukterfigs.htm, accessed 13 August 2006.

43 'Q and A: Anti-terrorism Legislation', BBC News, 17 October 2003, http://news.bbc.co.uk/1/hi/uk/3197394.stm, accessed 5 January 2007.

44 Denise Winterman, 'Belmarsh – Britain's Guantanamo Bay?', BBC News, 6 October 2004, http://news.bbc.co.uk/1/hi/magazine/3714864.stm, accessed 14 January 2006; Steve Crawshaw, 'Belmarsh Prison – Britain's Guantanamo-Lite', *Observer*, 4 July 2004; Liberty, 'High Court Appeal over Britain's Guantanamo', 5 July 2004, www.liberty-human-rights.org.uk/news-and-events/1-press-releases/2004/internment-appeal-july-04.shtml, accessed 14 January 2006.

45 'Terror Detainees Win Lords Appeal', BBC News, 16 December 2004, http://news.bbc.co.uk/1/hi/uk/4100481.stm, 1 May 2007.

46 Privy Counsellor Review Committee, 'Anti-Terrorism, Crime and Security 2001 Review: Report', 18 December 2003, www.archive2.official-documents.co.uk/document/deps/hc/hc100/100.pdf, accessed 13 December 2006; 'Charles Clarke Parliamentary Introduction of the Prevention of Terrorism Bill 2005', Home Office, 22 February 2005, http://press.homeoffice.gov.uk/Speeches/02-05-st-prevention-terrorism, accessed 19 March 2007; 'Opinions of the Lords of Appeal for Judgment in the Cause A (FC) and others (FC) (Appellants) v. Secretary of State for the Home Department (Respondent) and X (FC) and another (FC) (Appellants) v. Secretary of State for the Home Department (Respondent)', 16 December 2004, www.publications.parliament.uk/pa/ld200405/ldjudgmt/jd041216/a&others.pdf, accessed 14 May 2007; 'Who Are the Terror Detainees?' BBC News, 11 March 2005, http://news.bbc.co.uk/1/hi/uk/4101751.stm, accessed 12 March 2007.

47 Lord Hoffman, 'Opinions of the Lords of Appeal for Judgment in the Cause A (FC) and others (FC) (Appellants) v. Secretary of State for the Home Department (Respondent) and X (FC) and another (FC) (Appellants) v. Secretary of State for the Home Department (Respondent)', 16 December 2004, http://www.publications.parliament.uk/pa/ld200405/ldjudgmt/jd041216/a&others.pdf, accessed 14 May 2007.

48 Lord Carlile, 'Second Annual Report on the Prevention of Terrorism Act 2005', 19 February 2007, www.statewatch.org/news/2007/feb/uk-pta-carlile-ann-report.pdf, accessed 14 March 2007; see also 'Prevention of Terrorism Act 2005', www.opsi.gov.uk/ACTS/acts2005/50002—a.htm#1, accessed 8 January 2007.

49 'Charles Clarke Parliamentary Introduction of the Prevention of Terrorism Bill 2005.'

50 'Al-Qaeda Terrorists "on UK Streets".'

51 Tony Blair, as quoted in Oborne, *The Use and Abuse of Terror*, 1.

52 Tony Blair, as quoted in Peter Oborne, 'The Politics of Fear (Or How Tony Blair Misled us Over the War on Terror)', *Independent*, 15 February 2006.

53 Interview with Bob Milton, former senior Metropolitan Police Officer, *Today*, BBC Radio 4, 24 May 2007.

54 Martin Bright and Gaby Hinsliff, 'Chaos: How War on Terror Became a Political Dogfight', *Observer*, 13 March 2005.

55 Michael White and Vikram Dodd, 'New Terror Act Hit by "Teething Troubles"', *Guardian*, 14 March 2005; 'Secretary of State for the Home Department and MB', www.judiciary.gov.uk/docs/judgments_ guidance/control_order_mb_v_sshd_010806.pdf, accessed 24 May 2007; Fred Attewill, 'Reid Promises Tough Measures After Trio Vanish', *Guardian*, 24 May 2007.

56 Katherine Shrader, 'Report Says Iraq Problems Were Expected', *Washington Post*, 26 May 2007; Walter Pincus, 'Before War, CIA Warned of Negative Outcomes', *Washington Post*, 3 June 2007.

57 Australian Broadcasting Corporation, 'British Public Opinion Shifts to Support Iraq War', 3 April 2003, www.abc.net.au/lateline/content/2003/ s824112.htm, accessed 12 February 2007.

58 'Bird Flu "More Risk" than Terror', BBC News, 13 March 2005, http://news. bbc.co.uk/1/hi/england/london/4344787.stm, accessed 12 November 2006.

59 'Timeline of the 7 July Attacks', BBC News, 11 July 2006, http://news. bbc.co.uk/2/hi/uk_news/5032756.stm, accessed 10 April 2007.

60 'Terror Demands More Thought, Not Less', *New Statesman*, 15 August 2005; Oborne, *The Use and Abuse of Terror*, 2, 10, 11; Martin Bright, 'Losing the Plot', *New Statesman*, 30 January 2006.

61 Aluf Benn, Yossi Melman and Roni Singer, 'Ministers Reject Blair's Linkage of Bombings to Mideast Conflict', *Haaretz*, 23 July 2005.

62 'Tony Blair Press Conference.'

63 'Q&A: Terrorism Laws', BBC News, 3 July 2006, http://news.bbc.co.uk/ 1/hi/uk_politics/4715478.stm, accessed 15 December 2006.

64 'Terrorism Act 2006', 30 March 2006, www.opsi.gov.uk/acts/ en2006/2006en11.htm, accessed 9 April 2007.

65 'Gov't Bans Two Groups for Glorifying Terrorism', *Agence France Press*, 17 July 2006.

66 'Terrorism Act 2006'.

67 Alun Jones, Rupert Bowers and Hugo D. Lodge, *Blackstone's Guide to the Terrorism Act 2006* (Oxford and New York: Oxford University Press, 2006), 77; Shami Chakrabarti, 'This Would Be Internment', *Guardian*, 5 June 2007.

68 Deborah Orr, 'Do You Want Psychological Torture in Your Name?' *Independent*, 9 November 2005.

69 'Brown Plans New Anti-terror Laws', BBC News, 3 June 2007, http://news.bbc.co.uk/1/hi/uk_politics/6715885.stm, accessed 14 July 2007.

Chapter 3

1 Peter Taylor, 'Six Days that Shook Britain', *Guardian*, 24 July 2002.

2 George Crile, *Charlie Wilson's War: The Extraordinary Story of the Largest Covert Operation in History* (New York: Grove/Atlantic, 2004); Steve Coll, *Ghost Wars: The Secret History of the CIA, Afghanistan and Bin Laden* (London: Penguin, 2005); Marc Sageman, *Understanding Terror Networks* (Philadelphia: University of Pennsylvania Press, 2004), 1–59.

3 Bruce Lawrence (ed), *Messages to the World: The Statements of Osama bin Laden* (London: Verso, 2005), 23–30, 58–62, 61; Sageman, *Understanding Terror Networks*, 40–64.

4 For categories of terrorism see Bruce Hoffman, *Inside Terrorism* (New York: Columbia University Press, 2006), 40–88.

5 See, for example, the case of Algeria. Jason Burke, *Al-Qaeda: The True Story of Radical Islam* (London: Penguin Books, 2004), 200–3.

6 Benjamin Barber, *Jihad vs. McWorld* (New York: Corgi Adult, 2003), xv; Gilles Kepel, *The War for Muslim Minds: Islam and the West* (New York: Belknap Press, 2005), 123.

7 Anonymous [Michael Scheuer], *Imperial Hubris: Why the West is Losing the War on Terror* (Washington DC: Brassey's, 2004), 100. For more information on this angle see Michael Dunn, 'The "Clash of Civilizations" and the "War on Terror"', *49th Parallel*, vol. 20 (Winter 2006/7), 1–22.

8 Sageman, *Understanding Terror Networks*, 20–51.

9 'Bin Laden Applied for Asylum in UK', *People's Daily Online*, 30 September 2005, http://english.people.com.cn/200509/30/eng20050930_211800.html, accessed 12 December 2006; Sean O'Neill and Daniel McGrory, *The Suicide Factory: Abu Hamza and the Finsbury Park Mosque* (London: Harper Perennial, 2006), 111.

10 'Bomb Maker Jailed for 20 Years', BBC News, 27 February 2002, http://news.bbc.co.uk/1/hi/england/1845218.stm, accessed 15 June 2007; Michael Evans, 'Al-Qaeda Specialist Moves up to Take Top Post at Security Service', *The Times*, 8 March 2007.

11 Annie Machon, *Spies, Lies and Whistleblowers: MI5, MI6 and the Shayler Affair* (Sussex: The Book Guild, 2005), 228.

12 'Statistics on the Operation of Prevention of Terrorism Legislation for 2000', Home Office, 13 August 2001, www.homeoffice.gov.uk/rds/pdfs/hosb1601.pdf, accessed 14 February 2007. The year 2000 includes the first seven weeks of 2001 when the Terrorism Act 2000 replaced the Prevention of Terrorism Act.

13 Ibid.

14 Ibid.

15 Bernard Porter, *Plots and Paranoia: A History of Political Espionage in Britain, 1790–1988* (London and New York: Routledge, 1992), 91–3.

16 James Cusick, 'India Links Kidnapping of British Tourists to Pakistan', *Independent*, 8 November 1994.

17 Sean O'Neill, 'Why France Lived in Fear of "Londonistan"', *Daily Telegraph*,

13 October 2001; Elaine Sciolino and Don Van Natta Jr, 'For a Decade, London Thrived as a Busy Crossroads of Terror', *New York Times*, 10 July 2005; Kavita Suri, 'Radical Islam and British Muslims', *Kashmir Herald*, 7 July 2005; O'Neill and McGrory, *The Suicide Factory*, 103–22.

18 As quoted in Sciolino and Van Natta Jr., 'For a Decade'.

19 Robert Baer, *See No Evil: The True Story of a Ground Soldier in the CIA's War on Terrorism* (New York: Three Rivers Press, 2003), xv–xvi.

20 For the memoir of an individual involved in Hizb ut-Tahrir in the 1990s, see Ed Husain, *The Islamist* (London: Penguin Books, 2007).

21 Elliot Major Lee, 'Muslim Student Group Linked to Terrorist Attacks', *Guardian*, 19 September 2001; Anthony Glees and Chris Pope, *When Students Turn to Terror: Terrorist and Extremist Activity on British Campuses* (London: Social Affairs Unit, 2005), 44–7.

22 Sciolino and Van Natta Jr., 'For a Decade'.

23 Richard Norton-Taylor, 'Detained Leader Offered to Inform on Extremists', *Guardian*, 24 March 2004.

24 'Who Are the Terror Detainees?' BBC News, 11 March 2005, http://news.bbc.co.uk/1/hi/uk/4101751.stm, accessed 12 March 2007; 'Profile: Abu Qatada', BBC News, http://news.bbc.co.uk/1/hi/uk/4141594.stm, accessed 5 June 2007; Simon Jeffrey, 'Profile: Abu Qatada', *Guardian*, 11 August 2005.

25 Anouar Boukhars, 'The Challenge of Terrorism and Religious Extremism in Jordan', *Strategic Insights*, 5 (4) (April 2006), www.ccc. nps.navy.mil/si/2006/Apr/boukharsApr06.pdf, accessed 14 July 2007.

26 Melanie Phillips, *Londonistan: How Britain Is Creating a Terror State Within* (London: Gibson Square, 2006), 13.

27 David Stringer, 'London Police: Mosque a Terrorist Haven', *Associated Press*, 8 February 2006; 'UK Police Criticised for Abu Hamza Delay', *Turkish Daily News*, 9 February 2006; 'Radical British Muslim Cleric to Face U.S. Extradition Hearing in May', *Associated Press*, 31 January 2007; Mary Jordan, 'Fiery London Cleric Found Guilty', *Washington Post*, 8 February 2006.

28 Michael Gove, *Celsius 7/7: How the West's Policy of Appeasement Has Provoked Yet More Fundamentalist Terror – and What Has To Be Done Now* (London: Weidenfeld & Nicolson, 2006), 84–93; Phillips, *Londonistan*, 9–20.

29 Matthew Campbell and Jimmy Burns, 'Key Planks of Blair's Anti-Terror Plan Unfulfilled', *Financial Times*, 6 July 2006.

30 'Report: MI5 Sought to Recruit Al-Qaida Leader', *United Press International*, 27 July 2005.

31 Martin Bright and Paul Harris, '"Londonistan" No Longer Rings True', *Observer*, 17 July 2005.

32 Peter Clarke, 'Learning from Experience – Counter Terrorism in the UK since 9/11', Colin Cramphorn Memorial Lecture, 24 April 2007.

33 Terry McDermott, *Perfect Soldiers: The 9/11 Hijackers: Who They Were, Why They Did It* (New York: Harper Paperbacks, 2006).

34 For the most detailed account of the 11 September attacks, see 9/11 Com-
    mission, *The 9/11 Commission Report: Final Report of the National Com-
    mission on Terrorist Attacks Upon the United States* (New York: W. W.
    Norton & Company, 2004).

35 Clarke, 'Learning from Experience.'

36 O'Neill, 'Why France Lived'; Gregory F. Treverton, 'Terrorism, Intelligence
    and Law Enforcement: Learning the Right Lessons', *Intelligence and
    National Security,* 18 (4) (2003), 121–40.

37 For more on the transformation of the terrorist threat see Jytte Klausen,
    'Towards a Community-Based Approach to Counter-Terrorism', United
    States Institute of Peace, www.usip.org/pubs/usipeace_briefings/
    2007/0205_terrorism.html, accessed 14 April 2007.

38 Jeevan Vasagar and Vikram Dodd, 'British Muslims Take Path to Jihad',
    Guardian, 29 December 2000.

39 Dominic Casciani, 'Path to Extremism: How It Started', BBC News, 3 May
    2007, http://news.bbc.co.uk/1/hi/uk/6619147.stm, accessed 10 May
    2007; Vasagar and Dodd, 'British Muslims Take Path to Jihad'.

40 'Exchange Between Reid, Judge Follows Life Sentence', CNN, 6 December
    2003, www.cnn.com/2003/LAW/01/30/shoebomber.sentencing/, accessed
    1 May 2007.

41 'Terror Suspect Admits Plane Plot', BBC News, 28 February 2005,
    http://news.bbc.co.uk/1/hi/england/gloucestershire/4304223.stm, accessed
    6 April 2007; Jenny Booth, 'Gloucester Shoebomber Jailed for 13 Years',
    The Times, 22 April 2005.

42 Shiv Malik, 'New Statesman Profile – Omar Sharif', *New Statesman*,
    24 April 2006.

43 Clarke, 'Learning from Experience'.

44 'Government Response to the Intelligence and Security Committee's
    Report into the London Terrorist Attacks on 7 July 2005', May 2006,
    www.cabinetoffice.gov.uk/publications/reports/intelligence/govres_7july.pdf,
    accessed 14 March 2007.

45 John Steele, 'Home-Grown Threat That Unnerves US Allies', *Daily
    Telegraph*, 3 May 2007; Jonathan Milne, 'Ten Attempted Terror Attacks in
    London since 9/11, Says Mayor', *Guardian*, 27 December 2005.

46 Martin Bright and Jason Burke, 'Is There an Enemy Within?', *Observer*,
    27 February 2005; Jason Burke, 'Be Afraid, Perhaps. But Very Afraid? No',
    Observer, 13 March 2005.

47 'Measures to Combat Terrorism, Charles Clarke's Statement to the House',
    Home Office, 26 January 2005, http://press.homeoffice.gov.uk/
    Speeches/01-05-st-combat-terrorism, accessed 29 April 2007.

48 'How Terrorists Have Worked the System', *Daily Telegraph*, 21 March 2007.

49 'Police Terror Probe of Vast Scale', BBC News, 7 November 2006,
    http://news.bbc.co.uk/1/hi/uk/6125338.stm, accessed 12 May 2007;
    'Muslim Convert Who Plotted Terror', BBC News, 7 November 2006,
    http://news.bbc.co.uk/1/hi/uk/6121084.stm, accessed 12 May 2007;
    'Operation Rhyme Terror Convictions', Metropolitan Police, 15 June 2007,

http://cms.met.police.uk/news/convictions/terrorism/operation_rhyme_
terror_convictions, accessed 3 July 2007.

50 'N.Y. Man Admits He Aided Al Qaeda, Set up Jihad Camp', CNN, 11
August 2004, www.cnn.com/2004/LAW/08/11/ny.terror.suspect/, accessed
4 February 2007.

51 Peter Taylor, 'Real Spooks', *Panorama*, 30 April 2007, http://news.
bbc.co.uk/1/hi/programmes/panorama/6692741.stm, 1 July 2007.

52 Ibid.

53 'Profile: Omar Khyam', BBC News, 30 April 2007, http://news.bbc.co.uk/
1/hi/uk/6149794.stm, accessed 15 May 2007; Richard Smith, 'Bomb Plot's
Roots in Pakistan', BBC News, 30 April 2007, http://news.
bbc.co.uk/1/hi/uk/6172742.stm, accessed 15 June 2007.

54 Steele, 'Home-Grown Threat That Unnerves US Allies'.

55 Smith, 'Bomb Plot's Roots in Pakistan'; Casciani, 'Path to Extremism'.

56 'Fertiliser Plot Judge Asks for Majority Verdicts', *Guardian*, 20 April 2007.

57 Casciani, 'Path to Extremism'; Taylor, 'Real Spooks'; 'How Many More Are
Out There?' BBC Newsnight, 30 April 2007, http://news.bbc.co.uk/
1/hi/programmes/newsnight/6607647.stm, accessed 14 May 2007.

58 Casciani, 'Path to Extremism'; 'UK Fertilizer Bomb Plot', 2007,
http://news.bbc.co.uk/1/shared/spl/hi/guides/457000/457032/html/nn5page1.
stm, accessed 15 June 2007.

59 'Information Sought on British Man', *New York Times*, 8 July 2005; Vikram
Dodd, 'Moroccan Named by Newspapers as Suspect Condemns Attacks',
Guardian, 11 July 2005. Some among British Muslims also found it difficult
to accept what had happened. An opinion poll in 2007 found that 24 per
cent of British Muslims surveyed did not believe that the four men in
question had actually carried out the attacks. Mark Tran, 'Poll: Government
Had Role in July 7 Bombings', *Guardian*, 5 June 2007.

60 Taylor, 'Real Spooks'.

61 Mark Townsend, 'Leak Reveals Official Story of London Bombings',
Observer, 9 April 2006.

62 Shiv Malik, 'My Brother the Bomber', *Prospect*, June 2007; Glees and
Pope, *When Students Turn to Terror*, 30.

63 Aluf Benn, Yossi Melman and Roni Singer, 'Ministers Reject Blair's Linkage
of Bombings to Mideast Conflict', *Haaretz*, 23 July 2005; 'Tony Blair Press
Conference', 26 July 2005, www.number-10.gov.uk/output/Page7999.
asp, accessed 13 July 2007.

64 Glees and Pope, *When Students Turn to Terror*; Ian Sample, Matthew
Taylor and Polly Curtis, 'Foreign Scientists Barred Amid Terror Fears',
Guardian, 19 July 2005; Anthony Glees, 'Beacons of Truth or Crucibles of
Terror?' *Times Higher Education Supplement*, 23 September 2005.

65 Glees and Pope, *When Students Turn to Terror*, 35. Universities also could
potentially draw individuals away from radicalism. Ed Husain describes
how university lecturers contributed to his moving away from Islamic
extremism. Husain, *The Islamist*, 157–60.

66 Anes Alic, 'A Younger, Savvier Global Terror Cell', ISN Security Watch,

6 July 2006, www.isn.ethz.ch/news/sw/details.cfm?id=16349, accessed 14 June 2007; Vikram Dodd, 'Extremists Used Internet to Urge Muslims to Follow Bin Laden and Join Holy War, Court Told', *Guardian*, 24 April 2007.

67 Daniel McGrory, 'British Computer Whiz-Kid Exports Terror Via Internet', *Times*, 7 June 2006.

68 Charles Clarke, 'Contesting the Threat of Terrorism', Heritage Foundation, 21 October 2005, www.heritage.org/Research/HomelandSecurity/hl902.cfm, accessed 10 April 2007.

69 James Fallows, 'Bush's Lost Year', *Atlantic Monthly*, October 2004.

70 Colin Brown, '"War on Terror" Sends Wrong Message, Says Benn', *Independent*, 21 April 2007.

71 Hilary Benn, 'Where Does Development Fit in Foreign Policy?' Department of International Development, 16 April 2007, www.dfid.gov.uk/news/files/Speeches/foreign-policy-april07.asp, accessed 20 April 2007.

72 'London Bomber Video Aired on TV', BBC News, 2 September 2005, http://news.bbc.co.uk/1/hi/uk/4206708.stm, accessed 8 January 2007. According to Michael Gove, Khan's words are evidence that Iraq was not a significant part of the motivation for his terrorism. Gove, *Celsius 7/7*, 2.

73 'Transcript of Shehzad Tanweer Martyrdom Video', The Middle East Media Research Institute, 8 July 2006, www.memritv.org/Transcript.asp?P1=1186, accessed 10 November 2006.

74 Joint Intelligence Committee, 'International Terrorism: War with Iraq', as quoted in George Jones, 'Blair Rejected Terror Warnings', *Daily Telegraph*, 12 September 2003.

75 'Young Muslims and Extremism', Home Office and Foreign Office, 2004, www.globalsecurity.org/security/library/report/2004/muslimext-uk.htm#gfc, accessed 2 May 2007.

76 Martin Bright, 'Leak Shows Blair Told of Iraq War Terror Link', *Observer*, 28 August 2005; letter from Michael Jay to Sir Andrew Turnbull, 18 May 2004, http://politics.guardian.co.uk/foi/images/0,9069,1558170,00.html, accessed 14 July 2006.

77 Dana Priest, 'Iraq New Terror Breeding Ground', *Washington Post*, 14 January 2005.

78 David Leppard, 'Iraq Terror Backlash in UK "for Years"', *Sunday Times*, 2 April 2006.

79 MI5 website as quoted in Richard Norton-Taylor, 'MI5 Links Iraq to Extremists in UK', *Guardian*, 29 July 2005.

80 Police document as quoted in Vikram Dodd, 'Police Report: Foreign Policy Helped Make UK a Target', *Guardian*, 7 July 2006.

81 'Declassified Key Judgments of the National Intelligence Estimate [NIE]: Trends in Global Terrorism: Implications for the United States', April 2006, www.globalsecurity.org/intell/library/reports/2006/nie_global-terror-trends_apr2006.htm, accessed 3 July 2007.

82 For example, see Gove, *Celsius 7/7*, 76–8; Melanie Phillips, 'Still Behind the Terror Curve', *Daily Mail*, 2 July 2007.

83 'Blair Speech on Terror', BBC News, 16 July 2005, http://news.bbc.co.uk/

1/hi/uk/4689363.stm, accessed 8 November 2006.

84 Leppard, 'Iraq Terror Backlash in UK "for Years"'.

85 William Blum, *Rogue State: A Guide to the World's Only Superpower* (New York: Common Courage Press, 2005) 1–27, 127–67, 184–99.

86 Douglas Jehl, 'The Struggle for Iraq: Combatants; Iraq May Be Prime Place for Training of Militants, C.I.A. Report Concludes', *New York Times*, 22 June 2005.

87 Greg Miller, 'Influx of Al Qaeda, Money into Pakistan Is Seen', *L.A. Times*, 20 May 2007.

88 Dave Moniz and Steven Komarow, 'Shifts from bin Laden Hunt Invoke Questions', *USA Today*, 28 March 2004.

89 Peter Bergen and Paul Cruickshank, 'The Iraq Effect: War Has Increased Terrorism Sevenfold Worldwide', *Mother Jones*, 1 March 2007.

90 Tony Blair, 'Resignation Speech', *Guardian*, 10 May 2007.

91 'Al-Qaeda Terrorists "on UK Streets"', *Daily Telegraph*, 6 March 2005; Richard Norton-Taylor, 'Scaremongering', *Guardian*, 8 March 2005; Burke, 'Be Afraid'; Sciolino and Van Natta Jr, 'For a Decade'; Robert Winnett and David Leppard, 'Terror in London', *Times*, 10 July 2005; Richard Ford, 'MI5 Has Hundreds of Terror Suspects under Surveillance, Clarke Tells MPs', *The Times*, 14 September 2005; Peter Oborne, 'The Politics of Fear (Or How Tony Blair Misled us Over the War on Terror)', *Independent*, 15 February 2006; Jason Bennetto, 'MI5 Conducts Secret Inquiry into 8,000 Al-Qa'ida "Sympathisers"', *Independent*, 3 July 2006; Jason Bennetto, Colin Brown, Nigel Morris, and Kim Sengupta, 'Security Services Identify 700 Potential Al-Qa'ida Terrorists at Large in Britain', *Independent*, 10 May 2006; David Cracknell and David Leppard, 'Brown: I'll Be Terror Overlord', *Sunday Times*, 12 November 2006; Stephen Fidler, 'Britain under Threat from Resurgent Al-Qaeda Security Forces Warn That 1,600 Operatives Are Plotting Attacks Here and Abroad', *Financial Times*, 7 December 2006; John Steele, '4,000 Terror Suspects in UK', *Daily Telegraph*, 7 May 2007; Gordon Brown, 'Statement on Security', 25 July 2007, www.pm.gov.uk/output/Page12675.asp, accessed 27 July 2007.

92 Norton-Taylor, 'Scaremongering'.

93 Craig Whitlock, 'Terrorists Proving Harder to Profile: European Officials Say Traits of Suspected Islamic Extremists Are Constantly Shifting', *Washington Post*, 12 March 2007.

94 Debra Zedalis, *Female Suicide Bombers*, US Army War College, June 2004, www.strategicstudiesinstitute.army.mil/pdffiles/PUB408.pdf, accessed 10 June 2007; Vic Groskop, 'The Women with Death at their Fingertips – Martyrs or Victims?' *The Scotsman*, 5 September 2004; Anne Speckhard and Khapta Akhmedova, 'Black Widows: The Chechen Female Suicide Terrorists', in Yoram Schweitzer (ed.), *Female Suicide Bombers: Dying for Equality?* (Tel Aviv: Jaffee Center for Strategic Studies, 2006), 63–80, www.tau.ac.il/jcss/memoranda/memo84.pdf, accessed 11 June 2007.

95 'Declassified Key Judgments of the NIE'.

96 Brent Ellis, 'Countering Complexity: An Analytical Framework to Guide

Counter-Terrorism Policy-Making', in Russell D. Howard and Reid L. Sawyer (eds), *Terrorism and Counterterrorism: Understanding the New Security Environment* (New York: McGraw-Hill, 2003), 117.

97   Suri, 'Radical Islam and British Muslims'.

98   Bruce Riedel, 'Al Qaeda Strikes Back', *Foreign Affairs* 86 (3) (May/June 2007).

99   Angella Johnson, 'Muslim Terrorists "Recruited at UK Universities"', *Guardian*, 8 November 1994; Cusick, 'India Links Kidnapping of British Tourists to Pakistan'.

100   Glees and Pope, *When Students Turn to Terror*, 28.

101   Suri, 'Radical Islam and British Muslims'.

102   Claudio Franco, 'Profile of a Suicide Bomber', ISN Security Watch, 21 July 2005, www.isn.ethz.ch/news/sw/details.cfm?ID=12263, accessed 14 April 2006.

103   Riedel, 'Al Qaeda Strikes Back'.

104   Declan Walsh, 'Pakistan's Soldiers "Huddling in their Bases" in Tribal Regions', *Guardian*, 16 June 2007; Stephen Fidler, 'Britain under Threat from Resurgent Al-Qaeda Security Forces Warn That 1,600 Operatives Are Plotting Attacks Here and Abroad', *Financial Times*, 7 December 2006.

105   Fidler, 'Britain under Threat'.

106   Anonymous US official as quoted in Daniel McGrory, 'Kidnap Plot Suspect "Had Threatened to Have Soldier's Head Cut Off Before"', *The Times*, 3 February 2007; Michael Evans, 'New Clues Support Al-Qaeda Theory for London Bombing', *The Times*, 30 January 2006; Michael Evans, 'Shortage of Money Led to 7/7 Security Failures', *The Times*, 11 May 2006.

107   '"Britons Could Attack US"', Sky News, 6 April 2007, http://news.sky.com/skynews/article/0,,30000-1259477,00.html, accessed 10 June 2007; Matt Weaver, 'US "Wants British Pakistanis to Have Entry Visas"', *Guardian*, 2 May 2007.

108   'Declassified Key Judgments of the NIE'.

109   Brown, 'Statement on Security', 25 July 2007.

110   '500 Terror Attacks in EU in 2006 – but Only 1 by Islamists', *Spiegel Online*, 11 April 2007, www.spiegel.de/international/europe/0,1518,476599,00.html, accessed 12 May 2007.

Chapter 4

1   Ian Cobain, David Hencke and Richard Norton-Taylor, 'MI5 Told MPs on Eve of 7/7: No Imminent Terror Threat', *Guardian*, 9 January 2007.

2   Ian Blair, as quoted on *Today*, BBC Radio 4, 7 July 2005, www.bbc.co.uk/radio4/today/listenagain/ram/today2_blair_20050707.ram, accessed 14 March 2007.

3   Michael Evans, 'Terror Alert Downgraded, Then Attacks Came out of the Blue', *The Times*, 8 July 2005.

4   Elaine Sciolino and Don Van Natta Jr, 'For a Decade, London Thrived as a

Busy Crossroads of Terror', *New York Times*, 10 July 2005; Intelligence and Security Committee (ISC), 'Report into the London Terrorist Attacks on 7 July 2005', 30 March 2006, www.cabinetoffice.gov.uk/publications/reports/intelligence/isc_7july_report.pdf, accessed 18 February 2007. For more on the process of Joint Terrorism Analysis Centre (JTAC) threat assessments, see Crispin Black, *7-7: The London Bombs: What Went Wrong?* (London: Gibson Square, 2005), 37–8.

5　ISC, 'Report into the London Terrorist Attacks'.

6　Ibid.; Michael Evans, 'Shortage of Money Led to 7/7 Security Failures', *The Times*, 11 May 2006.

7　Shiv Malik, 'My Brother the Bomber', *Prospect*, June 2007; Peter Taylor, 'Real Spooks', *Panorama*, 30 April 2007, http://news.bbc.co.uk/1/hi/programmes/panorama/6692741.stm, accessed 19 June 2007.

8　Stella Rimington, *Open Secret: The Autobiography of the Former Director-General of MI5* (London: Arrow Books, 2002), 210–2.

9　'"Shaylergate" Explained', BBC News, 20 August 2000, http://news.bbc.co.uk/1/hi/uk/885588.stm, accessed 4 July 2007.

10　Mark Hollingsworth and Nick Fielding, *Defending the Realm: MI5 and the Shayler Affair* (London: André Deutsch, 1999), 117–8, 122.

11　Peter Wright, with Paul Greengrass, *Spycatcher: The Candid Autobiography of a Senior Intelligence Officer* (Richmond, Victoria: Heinemann Australia, 1987).

12　Alun Jones, Rupert Bowers and Hugo D. Lodge, *Blackstone's Guide to the Terrorism Act 2006* (Oxford and New York: Oxford University Press, 2006), 95.

13　Paul Wilkinson, *Terrorism Versus Democracy: The Liberal State Response* (Abingdon, Oxford and New York: Routledge, 2006), 74.

14　Bernard Porter, *Plots and Paranoia: A History of Political Espionage in Britain, 1790–1988* (London and New York: Routledge, 1992), 199.

15　Michael Jacobson, *The West at War: U.S. and European Counterterrorism Efforts, Post-September 11* (Washington DC: The Washington Institute for Near East Policy, 2006), 43–4.

16　Wilkinson, *Terrorism Versus Democracy*, 77–9.

17　Peter Clarke, 'Learning from Experience – Counter Terrorism in the UK since 9/11', Colin Cramphorn Memorial Lecture, 24 April 2007. For more on Peter Clarke see Duncan Campbell and Rosie Cowan, 'The Guardian Profile: Peter Clarke', *Guardian*, 29 July 2005.

18　Matthew Teague, 'Double Blind', *Atlantic Monthly*, April 2006.

19　ISC, 'Report for 2001–2', www.cabinetoffice.gov.uk/publications/reports/intelligence/Intelligence.pdf, accessed 15 May 2006.

20　Terrorism Act 2000, www.opsi.gov.uk/acts/acts2000/20000011.htm; Vikram Dodd and Alan Travis, 'Muslims Face Increased Stop and Search', *Guardian*, 2 March 2005. For an example of 'stop and search' in practice, see Nicky Samengo-Turner, '"New Labour's Police State"', *Spectator*, 24 December 2004.

21　Lawrence Wright, *The Looming Tower* (New York: Albert A. Knopf, 2006),

330–1, 340–2; 9/11 Commission, *The 9/11 Commission Report: Final Report of the National Commission on Terrorist Attacks Upon the United States* (New York: W. W. Norton & Company, 2004).

22 'Report Slams CIA for Iraq Intelligence Failures', CNN, 9 July 2004, www.cnn.com/2004/ALLPOLITICS/07/09/senate.intelligence/index.html, accessed 17 July 2007.

23 ISC, 'Report for 2001–2'.

24 MI5, 'Terrorism Act 2006 – Successful Disruptions and Prosecutions', 2007, www.mi5.gov.uk/output/Page557.html, accessed 14 May 2007.

25 Ian Sample, Matthew Taylor and Polly Curtis, 'Foreign Scientists Barred Amid Terror Fears', *Guardian*, 19 July 2005.

26 Clarke, 'Learning from Experience'.

27 Peter Chalk and William Rosenau, *'Confronting the 'Enemy Within': Security Intelligence, the Police, and Counterterrorism in Four Democracies* (Washington DC: Rand Corporation, 2004), 10; ISC, 'Report for 2001–2'.

28 ISC, 'Report for 2004–5', www.cabinetoffice.gov.uk/publications/reports/intelligence/iscannualreport.pdf, accessed 1 March 2007.

29 Paul Wilkinson and Frank Gregory, 'Riding Pillion for Tackling Terrorism Is a High-Risk Policy', ISP/NSC Briefing Paper, July 2005, www.chathamhouse.org.uk/pdf/research/niis/BPsecurity.pdf, accessed 10 May 2007; ISC, 'Report for 2002–3', www.cabinetoffice.gov.uk/publications/reports/intelligence/annualir0203.pdf, accessed 1 May 2007.

30 ISC, Annual Reports, 1997–2006, www.cabinetoffice.gov.uk/intelligence/annual_reports.asp, accessed 1 April 2007.

31 Chalk and Rosenau, *Confronting the 'Enemy Within'*, 11.

32 Sophie Goodchild and Paul Lashmar, 'MI5 Trains Supermarket Checkout Staff', *Independent on Sunday*, 4 March 2007; Francis Elliott, 'Secret Plans to Turn Staff into Police Informers', *The Times*, 21 May 2007.

33 ISC, 'Report for 2001–2'.

34 Jeffrey Richelson and Desmond Ball, *The Ties That Bind: Intelligence Cooperation Between the UK/USA Countries* (New York: Routledge, 1990).

35 'MI5's "Torture" Evidence Revealed', BBC News, 2 November 2005, http://newsvote.bbc.co.uk/mpapps/pagetools/print/news.bbc.co.uk/1/hi/uk_politics/4363254.stm, accessed 4 January 2007.

36 David Leigh and Rob Evans, '"National Interest" Halts Arms Corruption Inquiry', *Guardian*, 15 December 2006.

37 'Pakistan Emerges as Al Qaeda Safe Haven', CBS News, www.cbsnews.com/stories/2007/07/17/terror/main3065010.shtml, accessed 17 July 2007.

38 'Counter Terrorism Command', Metropolitan Police, 2007, www.met.police.uk/so/counter_terrorism.htm, accessed 14 May 2007.

39 Statewatch, 'UK: Metropolitan Police Special Branch (MPSB) to be Amalgamated with the Anti-Terrorism Branch to Form New Counter-Terrorist Branch', www.statewatch.org/news/2005/sep/06uk-special-branch.htm, accessed 14 May 2007; Jonathan Guthrie and Jimmy Burns, 'Raids Illustrate Task of Winning Over Muslims', *The Times*, 1 February 2007.

40 Wilkinson and Gregory, 'Riding Pillion'; 'Joint Terrorism Analysis Centre (JTAC)', MI5, 2007, www.mi5.gov.uk/output/Page421.html, accessed 6 April 2007.

41 'Appointment of Security and Intelligence Co-ordinator and Permanent Secretary, Cabinet Office', Prime Minister's Office, 2002, www.number-10.gov.uk/output/Page2583.asp, accessed 11 March 2007.

42 Michael Evans, 'Terror Alert Downgraded, Then Attacks Came Out Of The Blue', *The Times*, 8 July 2005; Richard Norton-Taylor and Oliver Burkeman, 'US-Style Terror Alerts for UK', *Guardian*, 17 April 2006.

43 John Reid as quoted in Philip Johnston, 'Reid Blasts Management Failures at Home Office', *Daily Telegraph*, 24 May 2006.

44 Alan Travis, 'Struggling Home Office Split up to Combat Terrorism', *Guardian*, 30 March 2007.

45 'MI5 Staff to Rise from 2,000 to 3,000 and Extra Money for Special Branch', Statewatch, 2004, www.statewatch.org/news/2004/feb/36-sb-mi5.htm, accessed 11 January 2007.

46 Michael Evans, 'Shortage of Money Led to 7/7 Security Failures', *The Times*, 11 May 2006.

47 Vikram Dodd and Richard Norton-Taylor, 'Al-Qaida Plan to Infiltrate MI5 Revealed', *Guardian*, 4 July 2006.

48 ISC, 'Report for 2004–5'; Richard Norton-Taylor, 'MI5 to Expand Regional Offices', *Guardian*, 8 November 2005.

49 Hazel Blears, 'The Tools to Combat Terrorism', Home Office, February 2005, http://press.homeoffice.gov.uk/Speeches/, accessed 22 March 2007.

50 'Secrets and Mysteries, *Analysis*, BBC Radio 4, 19 April 2007, http://news.bbc.co.uk/nol/shared/spl/hi/programmes/analysis/transcripts/19_04_07.txt, accessed 15 May 2007.

51 Wilkinson and Gregory, 'Riding Pillion'.

52 Dave Leppard, 'Labour's War on Terror Is Failing, Says Leaked Report', *Sunday Times*, 23 October 2005.

53 Robert Winnett and David Leppard, 'Leaked No. 10 Dossier Reveals Al-Qaeda's British Recruits', *The Times*, 10 July 2005; 'Young Muslims and Extremism', Home Office and Foreign Office, 2004, www.globalsecurity.org/security/library/report/2004/muslimext-uk.htm#gfc, accessed 2 May 2007.

54 Jason Bennetto, 'MI5 Conducts Secret Inquiry into 8,000 Al-Qa'ida "Sympathisers"', *Independent*, 3 July 2006; Vikram Dodd, 'Special Branch to Track Muslims Across UK', *Guardian*, 20 July 2005.

55 Michael Evans, 'More Britons Are Turning to Terror, Says MI5 Director', *The Times*, 10 November 2006.

56 Peter Clarke, as quoted in Taylor, 'Real Spooks'; Jeff Sallot, 'Canada Could Escape Attack, CSIS Says', *Globe and Mail*, 20 June 2006; Steve Hewitt, *Spying 101: The RCMP's Secret Activities at Canadian Universities, 1917–1997* (Toronto: University of Toronto Press, 2002), 73–4, 122.

57 'Secret Ceremony for Special Unit', *Guardian*, 3 September 2005; 'Executed: Anatomy of a Police Killing', *The Times*, 21 August 2005.

58 Taylor, 'Real Spooks'.

59 Stewart Tendler, 'Police Admit They Still Have No Clues Over 7/7 Bombers', *The Times*, 4 July 2006.

60 Stewart Tendler, 'Terrorism Alert Puts More Armed Police on the Streets', *The Times*, 9 March 2007; 'Police Anti-Terror Efforts at All-Time High', *Guardian*, 3 July 2006.

61 Michael Evans, 'Privacy Row as Checks on Phones and E-Mails Hit 439,000', *The Times*, 20 February 2007.

62 Vikram Dodd and Alan Travis, 'Muslims Face Increased Stop and Search', *Guardian*, 2 March 2005; Jytte Klausen, 'Towards a Community-Based Approach to Counter-Terrorism', United States Institute of Peace, www.usip.org/pubs/usipeace_briefings/2007/0205_terrorism.html, accessed 14 April 2007.

63 Paul Wilkinson, as quoted by FBI Director Robert Mueller in speech to Executives' Club of Chicago, 12 September 2006, http://www.fbi.gov/pressrel/speeches/mueller091206.htm, accessed 27 August 2007.

64 'Countering International Terrorism: The United Kingdom's Strategy', Home Office, 2006, http://security.homeoffice.gov.uk/news-publications/publication-search/general/Contest-Strategy?view=Binary, accessed 11 February 2007; Michael Jacobson, 'Combating Terrorist Financing in Europe: Gradual Progress', Washington Institute for Near East Policy, 26 March 2007, www.washingtoninstitute.org/templateC05.php?CID=2583, accessed 3 May 2007.

65 'Source: U.S., U.K. At Odds Over Timing Of Arrests', MSNBC, 14 August 2006, www.msnbc.msn.com/id/14320452/, 14 April 2007.

66 Jonathan Milne, 'Ten Attempted Terror Attacks in London since 9/11, Says Mayor', *Guardian*, 27 December 2005; Sean Rayment, 'Security Forces "Foil Another Terrorist Plot Every Six Weeks"', *Sunday Telegraph*, 4 February 2007.

67 'Focus: Executed: Anatomy of a Police Killing', *The Times*, 21 August 2005.

68 Andrew Alderson, Sean Rayment and Patrick Hennessy, 'Terror Cell "Was Planning Nerve Gas Attack on Capital"', *Daily Telegraph*, 4 June 2006.

69 'Police Criticised for Terror Raid', BBC News, 13 February 2007, http://news.bbc.co.uk/1/hi/uk/6356931.stm, accessed 15 March 2007; 'Forest Gate Report – Key Findings', BBC News, 3 August 2006, http://news.bbc.co.uk/1/hi/uk/5243356.stm, accessed 13 February 2007.

70 Gerri Peev, 'Five Remanded on Kidnap Plot Charges', *The Scotsman*, 10 February 2007.

71 'Half of Terror Suspects Released', BBC News, 17 July 2007, http://news.bbc.co.uk/1/hi/uk/6902522.stm, accessed 17 July 2007.

72 Nigel Morris, 'Less Than One in 20 Held under Anti-Terror Laws Is Charged', *Independent*, 6 March 2007; 'Terrorism and the Law', Home Office, www.homeoffice.gov.uk/security/terrorism-and-the-law/, accessed 18 July 2007; 'Man Charged over "Airport Bomb"', BBC News, 6 July 2007, http://news.bbc.co.uk/1/hi/uk/6278318.stm, accessed 10 July 2007.

73 Ibid.

74 David Leppard and Richard Woods. 'Spies "Hid" Bomber Tape from MPs', *Sunday Times*, 14 May 2006; Tom Hays, 'U.S. Says Informant Flagged London Bomber', *Associated Press*, 8 February 2006; Michael Evans, 'New Clues Support Al-Qaeda Theory for London Bombing', *The Times*, 30 January 2006; Anthony Barnett and Martin Bright, 'Ministers "Shocked" at MI5's Lack of Information', *Observer*, 2 October 2005; Evans, 'Terror Alert Downgraded'; Sciolino and Van Natta Jr, 'For a Decade'; Cobain, Hencke and Norton-Taylor, 'MI5 Told MPs on Eve of 7/7'.

75 Melanie Phillips, 'Still Behind the Terror Curve', *Daily Mail*, 2 July 2007.

Chapter 5

1 Peter Clarke, 'Learning from Experience – Counter Terrorism in the UK since 9/11', Colin Cramphorn Memorial Lecture, 24 April 2007.

2 Michael Evans, 'Recruit Muslim Spies In War On Terror, Urges New Security Chief', *The Times*, 9 July 2007.

3 Patrick Hennessy, 'Fight Against Terror Could Take 15 Years', *Sunday Telegraph*, 8 July 2007.

4 For example, see Home Office and Foreign Office, 'Young Muslims and Extremism', 2004, www.globalsecurity.org/security/library/report/2004/muslimext-uk.htm#gfc, accessed 20 December 2006.

5 Thomas R. Mockaitis, 'Winning Hearts and Minds in the "War on Terrorism"', in Thomas R. Mockaitis and Paul B. Rich (eds), *Grand Strategy in the War against Terrorism* (London and Portland: Frank Cass, 2003), 37; 'Identifying Radicalism Key to Thwarting Terrorism, Conference Told', ABC Sydney, 26 February 2007, www.abc.net.au/news/items/200702/1857612.htm?sydney, accessed 12 April 2007.

6 Paul Wilkinson, *Terrorism Versus Democracy: The Liberal State Response* (Abingdon, Oxford and New York: Routledge, 2006), 61.

7 'Secrets and Mysteries, *Analysis*, BBC Radio 4, 19 April 2007, http://news.bbc.co.uk/nol/shared/spl/hi/programmes/analysis/transcripts/19_04_07.txt, accessed 15 May 2007.

8 Phillip Johnston, 'MI5 Seeks "Older, Wiser Women"', *Daily Telegraph*, 10 May 2005; Michael Evans, 'More Britons Are Turning to Terror, Says MI5 Director', *The Times*, 10 November 2006; Barney Calman, 'Policing with Passion: Is the Met Police Still Prejudiced against Ethnic Minorities and Women?', *Evening Standard*, 10 July 2006; Martin Bright, 'Revealed: MI6 Plan to Infiltrate Extremists', *Observer*, 4 September 2005. For a discussion of the problem the CIA had in infiltrating al-Qaeda pre-9/11 see Reuel Marc Gerecht, 'The Counterterrorist Myth', *Atlantic Monthly*, July/August 2001.

9 Scott Shane and Andrea Zarate, 'F.B.I. Killed Plot in Talking Stage', *New York Times*, 24 June 2006; 'Informant Says Attacks on Canadians Are Legitimate in Afghanistan', *Globe and Mail*, 23 August 2006; 'Suspects in Army Base Terror Plot Are Held Without Bail', *New York Times*, 12 May 2007.

10 Stan A. Taylor and Daniel Snow, 'Cold War Spies: Why They Spied and How They Got Caught', *Intelligence and National Security* 12 (2) (1997), 101–25.

11 Sean Rayment, 'Young, Black, Female? You Could Be Just the Spy MI5 Is Looking For', *Daily Telegraph*, 16 July 2006.

12 'Britons Review Relations with Muslim Minority', Angus Reid Global Monitor, 10 January 2007, www.angus-reid.com/polls/index.cfm/fuseaction/viewItem/itemID/14342, accessed 11 March 2007.

13 Home Office and Foreign Office, 'Young Muslims and Extremism'.

14 Alexandra Frean and Rajeev Syal, 'Muslim Britain Split over "Martyrs" of 7/7', *The Times*, 4 July 2006.

15 Michael Binyon, 'Poll Reveals Muslims as Model Citizens', *The Times*, 17 April 2007.

16 Michael Gove, *Celsius 7/7: How The West's Policy of Appeasement Has Provoked Yet More Fundamentalist Terror – And What Has To Be Done Now* (London: Weidenfeld & Nicolson, 2006), 93–4. According to Gove, 31 per cent of British Muslims believe that western society is 'decadent and immoral'. Melanie Phillips describes Britain as 'a decadent society, weakened by alarming tendencies towards social and cultural suicide'. Melanie Phillips, *Londonistan: How Britain Is Creating a Terror State Within* (London: Gibson Square, 2006), 22.

17 'Research Reveals Muslim Pupils More Tolerant than Non-Muslims', University of Lancaster, http://domino.lancs.ac.uk/info/lunews.nsf/I/8B3629F578C06354802571FB003C4A24, accessed 8 July 2007; Home Office and Foreign Office, 'Young Muslims and Extremism'.

18 Vikram Dodd, 'Study Rejects Claim that Muslim Areas Harbour Terrorists', *Guardian*, 20 November 2006; Craig Whitlock, 'Terrorists Proving Harder to Profile: European Officials Say Traits of Suspected Islamic Extremists Are Constantly Shifting', *Washington Post*, 12 March 2007.

19 'UK's Image Has Worsened, Say Britons', Angus Reid Global Monitor, 12 April 2007, www.angus-reid.com/polls/index.cfm/fuseaction/viewItem/itemID/15369, accessed 28 April 2007; Damien McElroy, 'Britain Tarnished by Iraq War, Say Three Reports', *Daily Telegraph*, 12 April 2007; 'Guantanamo Sends the Wrong Signal to the Muslim World', *Der Spiegel*, 4 April 2007, www.spiegel.de/international/germany/0,1518,475676,00.html, accessed 4 May 2007.

20 David Rose, 'Using Terror to Fight Terror', *Observer*, 26 February 2006; ISC, 'The Handling of Detainees by UK Intelligence Personnel in Afghanistan, Guantanamo Bay and Iraq', 1 March 2005, www.cabinetoffice.gov.uk/publications/reports/intelligence/treatdetainees.pdf, accessed 10 May 2007; Moazzam Begg, with Victoria Brittain, *Enemy Combatant: The Terrifying True Story of a Briton in Guantanamo Bay* (London: Pocket Books, 2006), 208.

21 Hugh Muir, 'MacShane Faces Revolt over "Insult" to British Muslims', *Guardian*, 28 November 2003; George Galloway, *I'm Not the Only One* (London: Penguin, 2004), 145.

22 Vikram Dodd and Alan Travis, 'Muslims Face Increased Stop and Search',

Guardian, 2 March 2005.

23 Ibid.; 'Blair to Review Anti-Terror Power', *Yahoo News*, 22 February 2007.

24 Vikram Dodd, 'Study Rejects Claim that Muslim Areas Harbour Terrorists', *Guardian*, 20 November 2006.

25 Binyon, 'Poll Reveals Muslims as Model Citizens'.

26 Ibid.; 'Community Responses to the War on Terror', Institute for Race Relations, 16 September 2006, www.irr.org.uk/pdf/IRR_Briefing_No.3.pdf, accessed 3 January 2007.

27 Tarique Ghaffur, 'Sections of Muslim Britain in Denial About Extremism', *Sunday Times*, 2 July 2006; David Cameron, 'What I Learnt from My Stay with a Muslim Family', *Observer*, 13 May 2007. For more on Muslim perceptions of Islamophobia and the media, see Saied R. Ameli, Syed Mohammed Marandi, Samera Ahmed, Seyfeddin Kara and Arzu Merali, *The British Media and Muslim Representation: The Ideology of Demonisation* (London: Islamic Human Rights Commission, 2006).

28 Jamie Doward, 'Ministers "Failing to Reach Muslims"', *Guardian*, 3 December 2006.

29 Nigel Morris, 'Enemies of the State?' *Independent*, 15 December 2005.

30 Nigel Morris, 'Less Than One in 20 Held under Anti-Terror Laws Is Charged', *Independent*, 6 March 2007; 'Terrorism and the Law', Home Office, www.homeoffice.gov.uk/security/terrorism-and-the-law/, accessed 18 July 2007.

31 Jeevan Vasagar, 'Thousands March with Family Raided by Police', *Guardian*, 19 June 2006; Katherine Haddon, 'Released Ex-Terror Suspect Slams "Police State" for Muslims', *Agence France Presse*, 8 February 2007; Martin Bright and Jason Burke, 'Is There an Enemy Within?' *Observer*, 27 February 2005; 'Muslims under Attack, Says Peer', BBC News, 15 October 2006, http://news.bbc.co.uk/1/hi/uk/6052394.stm, accessed 26 February 2007; 'Community Responses to the War on Terror'.

32 '"Stop and Quiz" Comes Under Fire', BBC News, 27 May 2007, http://news.bbc.co.uk/1/hi/uk_politics/6696673.stm, accessed 7 July 2007.

33 Crispin Black as quoted in Peter Oborne, *The Use and Abuse of Terror: The Construction of a False Narrative on the Domestic Terror Threat Plus Indy Article* (London: Centre for Policy Studies, 2006), 35.

34 'Interview with Bob Milton', *Today*, BBC Radio 4, 24 May 2007.

35 'Young Muslims and Extremism'; Mockbul Ali, Confidential Internal Memo, 14 July 2005, http://image.guardian.co.uk/sys-files/Observer/documents/2005/09/04/Document1.pdf, accessed 10 December 2006; Bob Beckley, as quoted in Matthew Campbell and Jimmy Burns, 'Key Planks of Blair's Anti-Terror Plan Unfulfilled', *Financial Times*, 6 July 2006.

36 Home Office and Foreign Office, 'Young Muslims and Extremism'.

37 John Reid, 'Speech to Muslim Groups in East London', Home Office, 20 September 2006, http://press.homeoffice.gov.uk/Speeches/sp-muslim-group-20-09-06, 25 February 2007.

38 Hilary Benn, 'Where Does Development Fit in Foreign Policy?', Department for International Development, 16 April 2007, www.dfid.gov.uk/news/

files/Speeches/foreign-policy-april07.asp, accessed 25 April 2007.

39 'Dallying in Appeasement', *Washington Times*, 2 March 2007; Melanie
    Phillips, 'Britain's War Against . . .Well, You Know', *USA Today*, 10 July
    2007; 'Don't Say "Jihad"', *The Journal Editorial Report*, 9 July 2007,
    www.opinionjournal.com/jer/?id=110010310, accessed 10 July 2007.

40 Tony Blair Press Conference', 26 July 2005, www.number-10.gov.uk/
    output/Page7999.asp, accessed 11 July 2007.

41 Oborne, *The Use and Abuse of Terror*, 9–11.

42 'Preventing Extremism Together: Working Groups', Department of Com-
    munities and Local Government, October 2005, www.communities.
    gov.uk/pub/16/PreventingExtremismTogetherworkinggroupreportAugOct
    2005_id1502016.pdf, accessed 10 January 2007.

43 Dominic Casciani, 'Moves to Marginalise Extremists', BBC News, 5 April
    2007, http://news.bbc.co.uk/1/hi/uk_politics/6528305.stm, accessed 14
    June 2007.

44 Richard Alleyne, 'Kelly Seeks to Defuse Religious Extremism Row', *Daily
    Telegraph*, 17 October 2006; Alexander Blair and Dominic Kennedy,
    'Islamic Militants Face Purge in Schools and Universities', *The Times*, 16
    October 2006; Vikram Dodd, 'Universities Urged to Spy on Muslims',
    Guardian, 16 October 2006; Reid, 'Speech to Muslim Groups in East
    London'; David Leppard, 'Blair to Launch Spin Battalion against Al-Qaeda
    Propaganda', *Sunday Times*, 28 January 2007.

45 Jamie Doward, 'Ministers "Failing to Reach Muslims"', *Guardian*, 3 Dec-
    ember 2006; 'Bringing It Home: Community Based Approaches to
    Counter-Terrorism', Demos, 4 December 2006, www.demos.co.uk/
    publications/bringingithome, accessed 15 May 2007.

Conclusion

1 David Ignatius, 'When the "Bleed-Out" Begins', *Washington Post*, 5 July
   2007; Michael Abramowitz, 'Intelligence Puts Rationale for War on Shakier
   Ground', *Washington Post*, 18 July 2007; 'Terror Suspects: Bilal Abdulla –
   Wanted Revenge for His Friend Killed in Iraq', *Daily Mail*, 4 July 2007.

2 'British "Favour ID Cards"', Ipsos MORI, 23 April 2004, www.ipsos-
   mori.com/polls/2004/detica-top.shtml, accessed 6 July 2007; Deborah
   Orr, 'Do you Want Psychological Torture in Your Name?' *Independent*,
   9 November 2005.

3 Ros Coward, '"They Have Given Me Somebody Else's Voice – Blair's
   Voice"', *Guardian*, 10 November 2005.

4 Ros Taylor, 'Bold and Resolute Reid Returns to Haunt Uneasy Brown',
   Guardian, 5 July 2007.

5 Gordon Brown, *The World at One*, BBC Radio, 15 May 2007.

6 Jill Lawless, 'Britons Cheer Brown for Attacks Response', *Yahoo News*,
   3 July 2007, http://news.yahoo.com/s/ap/20070703/ap_on_re_eu/britain_
   testing_brown, accessed 6 July 2007; Simon Jenkins, 'We Are Offering the
   Terrorist a Megaphone for His Cause', *Guardian*, 4 July 2007.

Bibliography

News Sources

Agence France Press   The Guardian   Spiegel Online
Associated Press   Haaretz   Sunday Telegraph
BBC News   The Independent   Sunday Times
CNN   MSNBC   The Times
Daily Mail   New York Times   Washington Post
Daily Telegraph   Sky News

Selected Documents and Speeches

'Anti-Terrorism, Crime and Security Act 2001'. Cabinet Office, 14 December
    2001, http://www.opsi.gov.uk/acts/en2001/2001en24.htm.

Benn, Hilary. 'Where Does Development Fit in Foreign Policy?'. Department for
    International Development, 16 April 2007, http://www.dfid.gov.uk/news/
    files/Speeches/foreign-policy-april07.asp.

Blair, Tony. 'Press Conference'. Prime Minister's Office, 26 July 2005,
    http://www.number-10.gov.uk/output/Page7999.asp.

—— 'Press Conference'. Prime Minister's Office, 5 August 2005,
    http://www.number10.gov.uk/output/Page8041.asp.

Carlile, Lord. Annual Reviews of Anti-Terrorism Legislation. Home Office,
    http://www.homeoffice.gov.uk/security/terrorism-and-the-law/checks-on-
    laws2/?version=8.

Clarke, Charles. 'Contesting the Threat of Terrorism'. Heritage Foundation, 21
    October 2005, http://www.heritage.org/Research/HomelandSecurity/hl902.cfm.

Clarke, Peter. 'Learning from Experience – Counter Terrorism in the UK since
    9/11'. Colin Cramphorn Memorial Lecture, 24 April 2007.

Intelligence and Security Committee. Annual Reports, 1997–2006. Cabinet
    Office, http://www.cabinetoffice.gov.uk/intelligence/annual_reports.asp.

—— 'Report into the London Terrorist Attacks on 7 July 2005'. Cabinet Office,
    May 2006, http://www.cabinetoffice.gov.uk/intelligence/special_
    reports.asp.

'Declassified Key Judgments of the National Intelligence Estimate – Trends in
    Global Terrorism: Implications for the United States'. National Intelligence
    Estimate, April 2006, http://www.globalsecurity.org/intell/library/reports/
    2006/nie_global-terror-trends_apr2006.htm.

Home Office. 'Countering International Terrorism: The United Kingdom's Strategy'. Home Office, July 2006, http://security.homeoffice.gov.uk/ news-publications/publication-search/general/Contest-Strategy.

—— 'Preventing Extremism Together'. Home Office, November 2005, http:// security.homeoffice.gov.uk/counter-terrorism-strategy/preventing-extremism/.

Home Office and Foreign Office, 'Young Muslims and Extremism'. Home Office and Foreign Office, 2004, http://www.globalsecurity.org/security/ library/report/2004/muslimext-uk.htm#gfc.

'Prevention of Terrorism Act 2005'. Cabinet Office, 11 March 2005, http://www.opsi.gov.uk/ACTS/acts2005/20050002.htm.

Reid, John. 'Speech to Muslim Groups in East London'. Home Office, 20 September 2006, http://press.homeoffice.gov.uk/Speeches/sp-muslim-group-20-09-06.

'Terrorism Act 2000'. Cabinet Office, 19 February 2000, http://www. opsi.gov.uk/Acts/acts2000/20000011.htm.

'Terrorism Act 2006'. Cabinet Office, 30 March 2006, http://www. opsi.gov.uk/acts/acts2006/20060011.htm.

Books

Ameli, Saied R., Syed Mohammed Marandi, Samera Ahmed, Seyfeddin Kara and Arzu Merali. *The British Media and Muslim Representation: The Ideology of Demonisation*. London: Islamic Human Rights Commission, 2006.

Anonymous [Michael Scheuer]. *Through Our Enemies' Eyes: Osama Bin Laden, Radical Islam, and the Future of America*. Washington DC: Potomac Books, 2003.

Baer, Robert. *See No Evil: The True Story of a Ground Soldier in the CIA's War on Terrorism*. New York: Three Rivers Press, 2003.

Barber, Benjamin. *Jihad vs. Mcworld*. New York: Corgi Adult, 2003.

Begg, Moazzam, with Victoria Brittain. *Enemy Combatant: The Terrifying True Story of a Briton in Guantanamo*. London: Pocket Books, 2006.

Bell, J. Bowyer. *IRA Tactics & Targets*. Dublin: Poolbeg, 1993.

—— *The Secret Army: The IRA, 1916–1979*. Dublin: The Academy Press, 1979.

Bergen, Peter L. *The Osama Bin Laden I Know: An Oral History of Al Qaeda's Leader*. New York: Free Press, 2006.

Black, Crispin. *7-7: The London Bombs: What Went Wrong?* London: Gibson Square, 2005.

Blum, William. *Rogue State: A Guide to the World's Only Superpower*. New York: Common Courage Press, 2005.

Burke, Jason. *Al-Qaeda: The True Story of Radical Islam*. London: Penguin Books, 2004.

Chalk, Peter and William Rosenau. *Confronting the 'Enemy within': Security Intelligence, the Police, and Counterterrorism in Four Democracies*. Washington DC: Rand Corporation, 2004.

Clarke, Richard. *Against All Enemies*. New York: Free Press, 2004.

Coll, Steve. *Ghost Wars: The Secret History of the CIA, Afghanistan and Bin Laden*. London: Penguin, 2005.

Commission, 9/11. *The 9/11 Commission Report: Final Report of the National Commission on Terrorist Attacks Upon the United States*. New York: W. W. Norton & Company, 2004.

Coogan, Tim Pat. *The I.R.A.* London: HarperCollins, 2000.

—— *The Troubles: Ireland's Ordeal 1966–1996 and the Search for Peace*. London: Hutchinson, 1995.

Crile, George. *Charlie Wilson's War: The Extraordinary Story of the Largest Covert Operation in History*. New York: Grove/Atlantic, 2004.

Ellis, Peter Berresford. *A History of the Irish Working Class*. London: Pluto Press, 1985.

English, Richard. *Armed Struggle*. London: Macmillan, 2003.

Galloway, George. *I'm Not the Only One*. London: Penguin, 2004.

Geraghty, Tony. *The Irish War: The Military History of a Domestic Conflict*. London: HarperCollins, 1998.

Glees, Anthony and Chris Pope. *When Students Turn to Terror: Terrorist and Extremist Activity on British Campuses*. London: Social Affairs Unit, 2005.

Gove, Michael. *Celsius 7/7: How the West's Policy of Appeasement Has Provoked Yet More Fundamentalist Terror – and What Has to Be Done Now*. London: Weidenfeld & Nicolson, 2006.

Greer, Steven. *Supergrasses: Study in Anti-Terrorist Law Enforcement in Northern Ireland*. Oxford: Clarendon Press, 1995.

Hamill, Desmond. *Pig in the Middle: The Army in Northern Ireland, 1969–1986*. London: Methuen, 1986.

Hart, Peter. *The I.R.A. At War, 1916–1923*. Oxford and New York: Oxford University Press, 2003.

Hewitt, Steve. *Spying 101: The RCMP's Secret Activities at Canadian Universities, 1917–1997*. Toronto: University of Toronto Press, 2002.

Hoffman, Bruce. *Inside Terrorism*. New York: Columbia University Press, 2006.

Hollingsworth, Mark and Nick Fielding. *Defending the Realm: MI5 and the Shayler Affair*. London: André Deutsch, 1999.

Huntington, Samuel P. *The Clash of Civilizations and the Remaking of World Order*. New York: Free Press, 1996.

Husain, Ed. *The Islamist*. London: Penguin, 2007.

Ingram, Martin and Greg Harkin. *Stakeknife: Britain's Secret Agents in Ireland*. Dublin: The O'Brien Press, 2004.

Jackson, Alan A. *Ireland, 1798–1998: Politics and War*. Oxford: Blackwell, 1999.

Jacobson, Michael. *The West at War: U.S. and European Counterterrorism Efforts, Post-September 11*. Washington DC: The Washington Institute for Near East Policy, 2006.

Jones, Alun, Rupert Bowers and Hugo D. Lodge. *Blackstone's Guide to the Terrorism Act 2006*. Oxford and New York: Oxford University Press, 2006.

Kepel, Gilles. *The War for Muslim Minds: Islam and the West*. Translated by Pascale Ghazaleh. New York: Belknap Press, 2005.

Kitson, Frank. *Low Intensity Operations: Subversion, Insurgency, Peace-Keeping*. London: Faber and Faber, 1971.

Lawrence, Bruce (ed.). *Messages to the World: The Statements of Osama bin Laden*. London: Verso, 2005.

McDermott, Terry. *Perfect Soldiers: The 9/11 Hijackers: Who They Were, Why They Did It*. New York: Harper Paperbacks, 2006.

Machon, Annie. *Spies, Lies and Whistleblowers: MI5, MI6 and the Shayler Affair*. Sussex: The Book Guild, 2005.

Martin, David C. and John Walcott. *Best Laid Plans: The Inside Story of America's War against Terrorism*. New York: Harper & Row, 1988.

Mockaitis, Thomas R. *British Counterinsurgency in the Post-Imperial Era*. Manchester and New York: Manchester University Press, 1995.

Mueller, John. *Overblown: How Politicians and the Terrorism Industry Inflate National Security Threats, and Why We Believe Them*. New York: Free Press, 2006.

Oborne, Peter. *The Use and Abuse of Terror: The Construction of a False Narrative on the Domestic Terror Threat Plus Indy Article*. London: Centre for Policy Studies, 2006.

O'Neill, Sean and Daniel McGrory. *The Suicide Factory: Abu Hamza and the Finsbury Park Mosque*. London: Harper Perennial, 2006.

Pape, Robert. *Dying to Win: The Strategic Logic of Suicide Terrorism*. New York: Random House Trade Paperbacks, 2005.

Phillips, Melanie. *Londonistan: How Britain Is Creating a Terror State Within*. London: Gibson Square, 2006.

Porter, Bernard. *The Origins of the Vigilant State: The London Metropolitan Police Special Branch before the First World War*. London: Weidenfeld & Nicolson, 1987.

—— *Plots and Paranoia: A History of Political Espionage in Britain, 1790–1988*. London and New York: Routledge, 1992.

Reeve, Simon. *The New Jackals: Ramzi Yousef, Osama Bin Laden and the Future of Terrorism*. London: André Deutsch, 1999.

Richardson, Louise. *What Terrorists Want: Understanding the Terrorist Threat*. London: John Murray, 2006.

Richelson, Jeffrey and Desmond Ball. *The Ties That Bind: Intelligence Cooperation Between the UK/USA Countries*. New York: Routledge, 1990.

Rimington, Stella. *Open Secret: The Autobiography of the Former Director-General of MI5*. London: Arrow Books, 2002.

Sageman, Marc. *Understanding Terror Networks*. Philadelphia: University of Pennsylvania Press, 2004.

Taylor, Peter. *Brits: The War against the IRA*. London: Bloomsbury, 2002.

Tonge, Jonathan. *Northern Ireland*. London: Polity Press, 2005.

Urban, Mark. *Big Boys' Rules: The Bestselling Story of the SAS and the Secret Struggle against the IRA*. London: Faber and Faber, 1992.

Wilkinson, Paul. *Terrorism Versus Democracy: The Liberal State Response*. Abingdon, Oxford and New York: Routledge, 2006.

Wright, Lawrence. *The Looming Tower*. New York: Albert A. Knopf, 2006.

Wright, Peter, with Paul Greengrass. *Spycatcher: The Candid Autobiography of a Senior Intelligence Officer*. Richmond, Victoria: Heinemann Australia, 1987.

Articles and Chapters

Alic, Anes. 'A Younger, Savvier Global Terror Cell'. ISN Security Watch, 6 July 2006, www.isn.ethz.ch/news/sw/details.cfm?id=16349.

Bergen, Peter and Paul Cruickshank. 'The Iraq Effect: War Has Increased Terrorism Sevenfold Worldwide'. *Mother Jones*, 1 March 2007.

Boukhars, Anouar. 'The Challenge of Terrorism and Religious Extremism in Jordan'. *Strategic Insights*, 5 (4) (April 2006), www.ccc.nps.navy.mil/si/2006/Apr/boukharsApr06.pdf.

Bright, Martin. 'Losing the Plot'. *New Statesman*, 30 January 2006.

—— 'Will Justice Miscarry Again?' *New Statesman*, 5 November 2001.

Chomsky, Noam. 'Terror and Just Response'. *Znet*, 2 July 2002, www.zmag.org/content/showarticle.cfm?ItemID=2064.

Dunn, Michael. 'The "Clash of Civilizations" and the "War on Terror"', *49th Parallel*, vol. 20 (Winter 2006/7), 1–12.

Ellis, Brent. 'Countering Complexity: An Analytical Framework to Guide Counter-Terrorism Policy-Making', in Russell D. Howard and Reid L. Sawyer (eds). *Terrorism and Counterterrorism: Understanding the New Security Environment*. New York: McGraw-Hill, 2003.

Fallows, James. 'Bush's Lost Year'. *Atlantic Monthly*, October 2004.

Franco, Claudio. 'Profile of a Suicide Bomber'. ISN Security Watch, 21 July 2005, www.isn.ethz.ch/news/sw/details.cfm?ID=12263.

Gerecht, Reuel Marc. 'The Counterterrorist Myth'. *Atlantic Monthly*, July/August 2001.

Glees, Anthony. 'Beacons of Truth or Crucibles of Terror?' *Times Higher Education Supplement*, 23 September 2005.

Hassett, Michael. 'Irish Nationalists, the British Government and Anti-Terrorist Legislation'. Paper presented at the European Social Science History Conference, Amsterdam, 2006.

Jenkins, Brian. 'International Terrorism: A New Mode of Conflict', in David Carlton and Carlo Schaerf (eds), *International Terrorism and World Security*. London: Croom Helm, 1975.

—— 'Nuclear Terrorism and Its Consequences'. *Society*, July/August 1980.

Klausen, Jytte. 'Towards a Community-Based Approach to Counter-Terrorism'. United States Institute of Peace, www.usip.org/pubs/usipeace_briefings/2007/0205_terrorism.html.

Malik, Shiv. 'My Brother the Bomber'. *Prospect*, June 2007.

—— 'New Statesman Profile – Omar Sharif'. *New Statesman*, 24 April 2006.

Mockaitis, Thomas R. 'Winning Hearts and Minds in the "War on Terrorism"', in Thomas R. Mockaitis and Paul B. Rich (eds), *Grand Strategy in the War against Terrorism*. London and Portland: Frank Cass, 2003.

Nicholls, Colin. 'The UK Anti-Terrorism Crime and Security Act 2001: Too Much . . . Too Soon'. Commonwealth Human Rights Initiative, February 2002, www.humanrightsinitiative.org/publications/nl/articles/uk/uk_anti_terrorism _crime_security_act_2001.pdf.

O'Brien, Conor Cruise. 'Thinking About Terrorism'. *Atlantic Monthly*, June 1986.

Riedel, Bruce. 'Al Qaeda Strikes Back'. *Foreign Affairs*, 86 (3), May/June 2007.

Speckhard, Anne and Khapta Akhmedova, 'Black Widows: The Chechen Female Suicide Terrorists', in Yoram Schweitzer (ed.), *Female Suicide Bombers: Dying for Equality?* Tel Aviv: Jaffee Center for Strategic Studies, 2006.

Taylor, Stan A. and Daniel Snow. 'Cold War Spies: Why They Spied and How They Got Caught'. *Intelligence and National Security*, 12 (2) (1997).

Teague, Matthew. 'Double Blind'. *Atlantic Monthly*, April 2006.

Treverton, Gregory F. 'Terrorism, Intelligence and Law Enforcement: Learning the Right Lessons'. *Intelligence and National Security*, 18 (4) (2003).

Wilkinson, Paul and Frank Gregory. 'Riding Pillion for Tackling Terrorism Is a High-Risk Policy'. ISP/NSC Briefing Paper, July 2005.

Zagaris, Bruce. 'U.K. High Court Rules Two British Suspects Can Be Extradited to U.S.'. *International Enforcement Law Reporter*, 23 (21) (2007).

Zedalis, Debra. 'Female Suicide Bombers'. US Army War College, June 2004, www.strategicstudiesinstitute.army.mil/pdffiles/PUB408.pdf.

Websites
Cabinet Office, www.cabinetoffice.gov.uk.
Channel 4, www.channel4.com.
Conflict Archive on the Internet, http://cain.ulst.ac.uk/index.html.
Heritage Foundation, www.heritage.org.
Home Office, www.homeoffice.gov.uk.
Melanie Phillips' Blog, www.melaniephillips.com.
MI5, www.mi5.gov.uk.
Newsnight, http://news.bbc.co.uk/1/hi/programmes/newsnight.
Office of Public Sector Information, www.opsi.gov.uk/acts/acts2000/ 20000011.htm.
Panorama, http://news.bbc.co.uk/1/hi/programmes/panorama.
Prime Minister's Office, www.number10.gov.uk.
Statewatch, www.statewatch.org.
Today, www.bbc.co.uk/radio4/today/.
The World at One, www.bbc.co.uk/radio4/news/wato/.
White House, www.whitehouse.gov.

Index

Lightning Source UK Ltd.
Milton Keynes UK
UKHW02f0329220518
323001UK00009B/89/P

9 780826 499004